PRISONER OF ANOTHER WAR

PRISONER OF ANOTHER WAR

A Remarkable Journey of Healing
From Childhood Trauma

MARILYN MURRAY

PageMill Press

BERKELEY·CALIFORNIA

Prisoner of Another War:
A Remarkable Journey of Healing From Childhood Trauma

Printed in the United States of America

For information address
PageMill Press, P.O. Box 8147, Berkeley, California, 94707.

First Edition

Typeset in Trump Mediæval

For
my grandchildren,
B.J., JANELL, and ASHLEY.

BE FREE!

Editorial Note

The events in this story actually happened. The editors personally interviewed most of the principal figures in this story and obtained permission to use their names and the pertinent details of their stories. In order to protect the privacy of others, especially members of the immediate family, past and present, many details have been omitted. For purposes of confidentiality the names of Marilyn Murray's therapeutic clients have been changed and the case histories either modified or presented as composites. It must also be noted that quoted conversations in the pages that follow are not verbatim records, but have been rendered according to the best recollections of the author.

Contents

Introduction
Stitches and Shock

Have you ever had a bad accident in which you broke a bone or had a severe wound?

"Once I rolled my sports car. I was really smashed up, with compound fractures in both legs. I also broke my collarbone and a few ribs. I was sedated, and I really didn't feel anything for days. I still don't remember the accident or anything immediately after it."

"When I was about ten I was running with a glass in my hand and fell. My hand was cut deeply. I had to have more than thirty stitches, but it was hours before I felt the pain."

"I was wounded in Vietnam while serving as a company commander. I was standing in the front of a troop carrier one day when gunfire suddenly erupted, and I was consumed in a blinding flash of light. After returning fire, I looked down and saw my left hand lying in a pool of blood, motionless on the troop carrier bench. I watched my fingers move and my mind flashed, 'At least my arm's still connected!' But most of my bicep had been blown away by Vietcong anti-tank fire. I waited a long time for a helicopter. I didn't feel any pain for awhile. When it finally began, a medic gave me some morphine."

Each of these accounts, the last by one of my

therapists, Dr. Peter Danylchuk, has in common the reaction of physical shock and delayed pain. When a person is hurt physically, the body's defense system activates automatically. The mind does not consciously say, "Don't hurt!" The response that represses the pain happens instantaneously.

Most of us recognize that we have an innate physical defense mechanism that keeps us from feeling the full impact of physical pain when we are hurt. The delay of the sensation of pain allows the rest of the body to send energy where it is most needed. The shock deadens not only the physical pain but also the emotional reaction to the trauma.

The shock we experience is essential for our survival. It protects us until we are able to deal with the pain. Although necessary for our survival, the protective mechanism of shock is meant to be temporary. Pain is necessary. If we did not feel pain, we would not know we were hurt. For example, if your body did not feel pain, you might leave your hand on a hot stove and severely burn it. Pain can also signal us that we need help.

I believe we also have an emotional defense mechanism that protects us from feeling the full intensity of emotional pain. This can work in conjunction with physical shock at the time of a physical wound. But there are other times when the emotional shock mechanism alone can be activated.

When you suffer through the death of a loved one, it is normal to experience a numbness of your emotions. Often you do not feel the real impact of the loss for weeks or even months. This reaction is also common in times of war when many traumatic events are happening simultaneously. Under such circumstances, emotional shock can cause us to repress our memories. This is often noted in war veterans who suffer from post-traumatic stress disorder. Many victims of the Holocaust experienced a deadening of their feelings and a repression of their memories of the horrors they suffered.

But what about a painful experience which is not remembered, an experience about which the person has no knowledge, a hazy wisp of a memory which darts in and out of a dream or arises in a momentary flashback? What causes this kind of memory loss? Is it normal?

I believe it is normal—not only normal, but necessary for survival—for a time. Each time a person, especially a child, experiences something painful and is unable to release the feelings connected with that painful event within a short period of time, then that person buries the pain through an unconscious repression similar to physical shock.

It does not have to be a major trauma to cause such repression. Painful events can vary widely and include not only accidents and wartime experiences but also verbal, emotional, physical, and sexual abuse. How much is repressed and how deeply buried the memories vary widely from one person to another.

Just like physical shock, emotional shock is meant to be temporary. When emotional shock continues indefinitely, when it becomes chronic, it causes severe damage. If a physical wound is not attended, it can become infected and cause even more severe, sometimes life-threatening, damage.

In the same way, emotional pain that is denied or repressed by chronic shock will take its toll some time, some place. An emotional wound will fester and either erupt or be driven underground to emerge in other ways.

Emotional "infection" can be revealed in destructive behaviors, addictions, depression, broken relationships, and physical pain. It can emerge even in so-called appropriate patterns of behavior, such as being a perfectionist, a workaholic, or an excessive caretaker.

In my work, as I speak to professionals and lay people on the subject of childhood trauma and abuse, I see multitudes of hurting people. These people are victims of war—not just the acknowledged wars of World War II, Korea, Vietnam, the Gulf. I hear stories over and over from victims of another war: one that occurs repeatedly in quiet bedrooms, on playgrounds, in schools and parks, and in vacant lots of a city like Wichita, Kansas. This war has no geographical boundaries. This war is not limited to a particular race, age, sex, class, or creed.

Not all the victims of this other war are as easily identified as those of Dachau or Da Nang. They do not bear numbers tattooed on their arms or have scars that serve as mute reminders of a bullet ripping through a shoulder or a thigh. These are the unidentified victims of a war that rages unchecked in every village, town, and city worldwide. These victims become prisoners of another war, imprisoned by the pains of their past. They are locked in cells of solitary confinement in the hidden caverns of their minds—in prisons as total and complete as those made of concrete and steel.

*This is the story of
one prisoner's struggle to be free.*

*The story is true.
The prisoner is me.*

Part One

Creating the Controlling Child

◆ 1 ◆

Wartime—1944

Wichita, Kansas, was a silent battleground, unlike the steamy jungles of Luzon or Mindanao or the snow-covered villages and cities of Lidice or Warsaw. Stark black-and-white images of uniformed bodies strewn carelessly in the snow flashed across movie screens, imprinting themselves into the memories of the citizens of Wichita: citizens who did not want to hear vague rumors of places like Buchenwald and Auschwitz, places where hollow-eyed children stood peering lifelessly through never-ending strands of barbed wire.

The snow-covered ground of Kansas had never been stained with the blood of soldiers fighting to defend her from foreign invaders. Her afternoon air had never heard the screams of a child being tortured by concentration camp guards.

But pain and war did exist.

Even in Kansas.

◆ ◆ ◆

"Momma! I can't breathe! Oh Momma, stay with me. I hate the dream. It scares me so."

"Shhh," came my mother's reply. "Momma's here honey."

"It feels like I'm drowning in white glue. There's sticky stuff on my face." I was choking, coughing, trying to breathe.

"Please Momma, just hold my hand and keep me awake so I won't have the dream."

♦ ♦ ♦

By all accounts, I had a perfect childhood. As an only child for eight years, I was surrounded by love and attention from both my parents. Although some of the attention shifted from me when my little sister was born, I still felt the caring and love of my family. My parents worked hard to provide for us. During the Depression we often moved to enable my father to find an available job. Lonely nights rocking a sleeping child were common for my mother.

Both my grandmothers died early and violently, but the family's grief over those deaths was never allowed to surface. Expressing strong feelings was not appropriate, especially if the feelings were considered to be weak or negative. One smiled, no matter how faintly, and went on.

My mother seemed determined that I have only "happy memories." Anger was always a big no-no. I cannot remember ever hearing my parents argue. "Peace at any price" was the unspoken rule. This protective environment, while well-intentioned, kept me naive and unaware of harsh realities. My exposure to violence was limited to a Saturday matinee watching Roy Rogers in a barroom fight.

I was taught, by both my parents and the community, that I would be judged by the way I looked and by the way I behaved. The Kansas state motto seemed to be, "What will other people think?" I was never to do anything unseemly, anything that would bring shame on me and on my family.

After the Depression, my parents returned to their small hometown of Marion, Kansas. But in 1944 we moved to Wichita for nine months while my father worked for the war effort. When the war was over, we returned to Marion, and I was delighted. I had not liked Wichita.

Back in Marion, I lived what seemed an idyllic, carefree life of hours playing by the river, taking long bike rides to the lake, riding horseback in the open fields, and attending church ice-cream socials in the park. True to Bible-Belt tradition, I attended church with my parents every Sunday. On holidays and other special occasions I enjoyed our large extended family, and the bountiful dinners prepared by myriads of aunts and cousins.

It did indeed seem perfect. But that terrifying dream plagued me throughout my childhood years—a nightmare always accompanied by a painful asthma attack, the asthma that had started so suddenly one winter night when I was eight.

My asthma kept me from participating in many physical activities. Although I was not particularly sickly, I had to eat special foods, take naps, and miss out on summer camp with the other kids. Since I could not compete physically, I competed intellectually and drove myself to become a straight "A" student.

My inseparable friend was a lively bubble named

Ginger. She was the crazy, fun one and I, the more dominant, sometimes serious, one. We organized school events, picnics, slumber parties, and double dates. I have wonderful memories of spending nights singing in harmony old campfire songs, like "Tell Me Why," or new ones, like "You'll Never Walk Alone." In my friendship with Ginger, I felt secure.

Despite our pledges of eternal loyalty, conflicts arose. Ginger was more carefree than I was, less burdened with "shoulds" and "oughts." I disapproved of her new "out-of-town" boyfriends. We drifted apart. One day I received a letter from her, asking my forgiveness and stating that I would always be the most special friend in her life. I cried for hours—something rare for me. But I never answered or even acknowledged her letter.

Instead, I focused on my final month of high school. Just before our senior trip, I had another asthma attack. I went on the trip, but I spent the entire time alone in my cabin, fighting to breathe.

Back home in Marion, the asthma continued. I got out of bed only long enough to attend my graduation. The next day, friends of the family who were visiting from Arizona told my parents of the clean mountain air there. They said that it was especially helpful for people with asthma. They invited me to come to Arizona for the summer.

Arizona? I was not certain where it was on the map. All I knew was that it was certainly far removed from Kansas.

In Kansas I lived within strictly prescribed boundaries, limits established by my culture, my generation, and my heritage. I never questioned those boundaries. They were there to keep me safe and protected from "bad things." Bad things happened to other persons in faraway places, far outside the safety of my sheltered environment.

But now, just nine days out of high school, excited and apprehensive, with $15 tucked in my pocket, I boarded a train for Arizona and said goodbye to the boundaries that controlled and confined my existence, and I said hello to a new frontier and a new life.

♦ 2 ♦

Freedom and Burial

Arizona did offer me a new life.

When I closed my eyes against the bright sun and breathed the fresh mountain air into my fluid-clogged lungs, I knew I was going to be free of my asthma once and for all. Yes, I thought, I am going to get well.

My summer visit to Arizona soon became a permanent move. Instead of returning to Kansas to go to college, I found work and a place of my own. My parents were so impressed with the physical change in me, for my asthma had disappeared as promised, that a year later they decided to move to Arizona. After they arrived, I moved in with them, no longer a girl but now their mature, adult daughter.

I had a job working in a western clothing factory, where the owner, Jack Mims, took me under his wing and began to teach me about the clothing business: merchandising, advertising, and sales. It was in one of his stores, where I was working as manager, that I first met my husband-to-be, Todd. Todd was handsome, charming, and a lay pastor at a small mission church. Within three weeks we were engaged. Our entire courtship was church oriented. I played the piano at the mission church, and we attended all church functions together.

On Easter Day 1956, we were married. The happiness of that day was soon overshadowed by an old enemy. Within a few days of the ceremony, I was hospitalized because of a severe asthma attack. The return of the asthma surprised me, and I could not imagine what had triggered it.

Soon after I returned home from the hospital, my mother came for a visit. She and Todd sat by my bedside as she told me that my dear friend Ginger had been killed in a car accident. I began to sob as I repeated over and over, "But, I loved her so much." I cried for all the memories and for the guilt I felt in not accepting her for who she was. As I lay in bed exhausted, I vowed I would never again feel that strongly about a friend. It hurt too much.

Soon after we were married, Todd and I moved to Phoenix so that he could return to college. I took a full-time job and began night classes in music and religious education. Todd and I also lay-pastored a small ranch church and drove six hours round-trip every Sunday. It was an exciting but exhausting time for both of us.

Three years after we had married, I became pregnant with our first child. On January 22, 1960, I gave birth to a bright-eyed little girl; we named her Jinger Janell. She lost no time in becoming the delight of our lives.

Todd turned his hand to retailing, using his charm, friendliness, and sales ability to build a loyal clientele in the then small town of Scottsdale, a suburb of Phoenix. In his spare time he went hunting with his parents and younger brothers. I knew when I married Todd that hunting and fishing were a major part of his existence. I accepted this arrangement as part of the marriage package. I was not aware at the time that these trips would become nearly the most important thing in his life. When I went into labor with our second child, Missy, Todd took me to the hospital, waited for the baby to arrive, and then left to go hunting.

Three months before Missy's birth, the western store where Todd was employed suddenly went bankrupt. With two children to support and many impending bills, Todd and I needed to make an immediate decision about our future. With our common backgrounds in western retailing, coupled with Todd's loyal following in Scottsdale, we decided to open our own western store. We opened for business on a cold January day in 1963, with not enough money in the cash register to change a five-dollar bill. We had a small tract house, but out of necessity, the store became home for us. I cooked hot dogs and soup for Jinger and Todd on a hot plate in the back room. I nursed Missy there too, often stopping in the middle to take care of a customer.

My sister, Mary Sue, was now married to Wayne Watson and had two boys, Tim and Randy, almost the same ages as our girls. Mary Sue often took care of Jinger and Missy while I worked and became a second mom to them; the four little ones were more like siblings than cousins. Vacations, holidays, and fun times with the Watsons and our extended families became important to all of us.

The ensuing years were busy and often difficult. With our schedule at the store, church activities, social and civic commitments, and raising two small girls, Todd and I seldom had time alone. When we were alone our conversation almost always centered around store business.

At night, after the girls were asleep, Todd often went to a meeting while I worked on the store books. When I looked in on Jinger and Missy, sleeping so peacefully, I envied their peace. I loved and enjoyed my little girls. I loved their spontaneous laughter. Reflecting on them and how much I loved them, I became aware of a loss within myself. The lively, expectant girl that arrived from Kansas was gone. I felt as if I had buried her.

I was drained and tired, but I thought I had no right to complain. I had been raised on the maxim, "Joy is spelled *Jesus, Others,* and *You.*" But its original context had become distorted. The maxim had come to mean that it was my duty, my role, to give sacrificially of myself to my family, my church, and my friends. To consider my own needs was not within my comprehension.

I rejected any fleeting feelings of resentment or frustration in my marriage or in any other aspect of my life. I had no model or terminology with which to measure my feelings. The term "codependent" was not in use. I loved my children, and I loved my husband. Everyone else thought we had it all, and I believed it. Whenever I had any feelings to indicate otherwise, I dismissed them as "selfish" and focused on my responsibilities to other people. I created a whirlwind of activity. The busier I became, the less time I had to feel.

Todd also filled his life with busyness. He never hesitated to give of himself to others. Gradually we began to travel two separate paths. Todd had the store, his friends, his adored children, his hunting trips, and his trail rides. I had my daughters, my church activities, the store to tend, and endless pages of bookkeeping.

No one noticed the growing distance between us; we were not even aware of it ourselves. We were two people walking side by side, but we were both looking outward, trying to take care of the rest of the world. We never turned, faced each other, and looked at our own needs. Neither of us knew that it was possible to learn to identify what *we* needed emotionally or that we had the *right* to ask for those needs to be met.

Avoiding conflict had always been important to me: do whatever is necessary to keep the peace. Business and family problems were rarely solved appropriately. If Todd vented his anger, I shut down. If I attempted to discuss a problem, he left. The next day, we acted as if the previous day's hurt and anger had never occurred.

Despite our communication difficulties, Todd and I had many wonderful times together, times that centered around our family and our rapidly growing business. Our store was a gathering place for local businessmen, ranchers and tourists. They loved the Old West atmosphere that Todd created. He also became known as one of the best horse traders around. He traded guns, western clothing, saddles, and art. If he had need of something, he traded for it. Our accountant thought he would go crazy trying to sort through the trades so that he could enter them in the books.

Todd and I were both interested in western art,

and many well-known artists in that field began to shop at our store. Occasionally some of them would bring paintings or bronzes to display for sale. Todd often traded for a small work for ourselves, and our interest increased with each new piece we acquired.

One day a wealthy rancher came in to pick up his felt hat, which we had sent away to be cleaned. As Todd steamed the crease back in his hat, the rancher reached over the counter and picked up a bronze statue of a cowboy. The rancher asked Todd about it, and Todd told him the story behind the bronze. The rancher then asked the price, and Todd replied, "Seventeen-fifty."

The rancher took his old hat from Todd, put it on his head, tucked the bronze under his sweat-stained, denim-covered arm, and walked to the door. Just as he exited, he turned and said, "Bill me." Todd was aghast. "Do you suppose he thinks I meant seventeen dollars and fifty cents?" A few days later, when a check arrived for seventeen hundred and fifty dollars, Todd made a statement that would change our lives:

"Honey, we're in the wrong business!"

◆ 3 ◆

Paintings and Prisons

In the late sixties Todd and I sold the store and opened an art gallery. Our timing was perfect, and we rode the crest of the surging interest in contemporary western art. Soon after we opened the gallery, Todd decided to take time off from work to raise money for a new Christian academy in our area.

I loved being in charge of the gallery. I worked closely with the artists and customers and established gallery policy. For the first time in many years, I had the opportunity to be creative and to become a whole person separate from Todd.

When Todd returned to the gallery two years later, I stepped back into my "proper" place as "Mrs. Todd." On the surface, I appeared to do so willingly, because I believed my role in life was to support Todd and encourage him to do what he wanted. I had been taught to bury myself and to expend my energy on making life smooth for my husband. I believed a woman's needs took last place behind the needs of everyone else around her.

As I continued working in the gallery, I surrounded myself with paintings. I was drawn to paintings of someone imprisoned—an Indian infant encased in tightly wound blankets, a lone rider encircled by the driving snow of a blizzard, a cowboy boxed in by canyon walls or surrounded by attacking Indians—paintings of confinement, and the search for release.

I had left the boundaries of Kansas to reach a new frontier in my life. But even geographical frontiers lose their sense of freedom and spontaneity with time. Eventually you realize that you have brought your old boundaries with you, or you create new ones. The fences I had brought with me were fortified by current experiences until they became high walls: walls that kept others from seeing who I really was, imprisoning walls that kept me from reaching out to anyone.

Within those walls was a person in physical pain. My asthma had been replaced with constant severe headaches, digestive problems, and leg and back pains. My mother had suffered from migraines when I was a child and had a long history of crippling arthritis. I thought head and body pain were relatively normal, especially for a woman. I consulted doctors, specialists, and nutritionists and tried acupressure, acupuncture, and biofeedback, but nothing relieved the pain. No one could even identify its source.

I hid the pain from others. I had to be cheerful and happy. I had work to do and people to care for. I entertained clients, church friends, and family, but always in the role of Todd's wife. I had no social life of my own. Finally, after I had declined several previous invitations, and with encouragement from Todd, I went on an all-women trail ride for a week.

It was the first time in fifteen years that I had been away from my husband and children.

What I found on that ride was companionship. I admired the independent, self-sufficient women riding with me. The guilt I felt in leaving my family to fend for themselves soon gave way to the warmth and fun this new companionship offered me. At night, we sang by the fire, while one of the women, Kay, played a guitar. Singing harmony with Kay reminded me of the songs I sang with Ginger—"My Buddy," "You Tell Me Your Dream." The memories were both happy and painful. When Kay and I sang "You'll Never Walk Alone," the words stuck in my throat as I fought back the tears.

As the days passed, Kay and I spent long hours in conversation around the campfire or while riding side by side. We both loved horses, music, and art; she was a sharp, successful businesswoman, and she had headaches as severe as mine. Although we shared these common interests, we were drastic opposites in everything else. Kay was raised in a strict, nondemonstrative home, and I was raised in a close family atmosphere. To Kay, religion was a crutch for the weak. To me it was my whole life. Despite these differences, I was intrigued by Kay.

In the ensuing months, as Kay and I spent more time together, I knew I was slipping away from my ideal of always being available for Todd, but something drew me forcefully toward the friendship. I had not allowed myself to experience emotional intimacy with a female friend since Ginger and I had drifted apart in high school. I thought that maybe now I could take that risk.

I received encouragement and support from Kay,

plus an understanding of my physical pain. Gradually I began to prefer my friendship with her to my surface relationship with Todd.

My work in the gallery and my friendship with Kay brought me the opportunity for creativity and companionship. Two trips to Europe with Todd as guests of friends gave me a different vision. As we traveled, I became aware for the first time of the personal devastation of war. Thirty years had not dimmed people's memories of being hungry or afraid. We visited Dachau, and there I saw huge photos of hollow-eyed children staring through barbed wire fences. Something happened to me as I looked at those eyes, something that went beyond the horror of that place and that time.

We went behind the Iron Curtain to Czechoslovakia. There we met Milos Solc, an elderly pastor with whom I felt an instant bond. As he shared the pain of his childhood poverty, abuse, and neglect and the torment of the war and the present Communist occupation, I touched a part of his pain that was my own. I felt "at home." Despite the miserable situation in Czechoslovakia at that time, I was almost tempted to stay.

As Todd and I returned to our world of reality, western art sales were booming. Oil prices were high, and oil men and bankers were among our biggest customers. A national art show that I produced at one of the country's largest western art museums, plus our many shows in Scottsdale, established me as a professional in my field. By age thirty-nine, I was one of the best-known female western art dealers in the country.

Acquaintances saw me as a "put-together"

woman with business and social success, an elegant home, a happy marriage, and beautiful teenage daughters. Yet something was wrong.

Something inside me screamed for my attention, screamed to be faced, heard, and understood. It ripped at my insides and tore at my head. Instead of listening, I worked harder and faster. With each new project, my pain level increased, as did my medication, which became less and less effective in my struggle to be released from my prison of pain. My freedom, however, would not come in the manner I had expected. As with most escapes, I would find a difficult journey.

And when I did break away, I would return again and again to the prison, for it was there that I felt the safest, the most secure.

♦ 4 ♦

More Than Friends

By 1975, Kay and I had become close friends. She was in the midst of a tumultuous marriage, and her life was crumbling around her. Looking for answers, she began to read a book called *The Art of Understanding Yourself* by Dr. Cecil Osborne. The first time she had looked through the book, she had seen the word *God* mentioned and had tossed the book aside. Now it held her interest. As a result of the book and counseling sessions, Kay began to make radical changes in her life.

I could hardly believe those changes. I immediately went to the nearest bookstore for a copy of Dr. Osborne's book. Each day, Kay and I would read a portion of the book, then get together to discuss it. Dr. Osborne wrote about a concept that was new to both of us: support groups, groups in which people share everyday problems with loving, caring, nonjudgmental friends.

That was the beginning of MORE THAN FRIENDS. Kay and I gathered a diverse group of women of various ages, marital status, and religious backgrounds. Kay called every woman she could think of and invited them to join.

Our group met once a week. During the meetings, I listened and encouraged others, but despite my attempts to share parts of myself, I could not talk about the things that hurt me deeply. I would tell Kay, but hold back in the group. Learning to be a "receiver" was very difficult for me. I could not break my compulsive pattern of giving long enough to allow others to be concerned for me and to show it. Unconsciously, I was refusing to tarnish the Murray family image.

Slowly I acknowledged within myself that I needed to change. I had never thought of myself as having needs or of the necessity of working on self-improvement. It seemed far too selfish to attend to any of my needs—emotional or otherwise.

At first, I held preconceived judgments and critical attitudes toward some of the other women in the group. I was reacting to them just as I had to Ginger's friends in high school. But as I listened to their stories, as I heard them share themselves with the group, I began to let go of the judgments and criticism. I also began to share some of myself. However, I would talk about myself only after everyone else had a turn and then only if there was time.

Life changes in the group were immediate. As a result, Kay and I received many inquiries from other women wanting to join as soon as possible. Eventually I resigned from working at the gallery and concentrated on setting up more groups. Todd seemed pleased that I was doing something more "spiritual" with my life.

During this time, Todd and I found our family to be a major source of joy. Jinger had married her high school sweetheart, Brad Richardson whose parents were close friends with my sister Mary Sue and her husband, Wayne; Missy was attending college in California but visited us regularly; the Watsons had added a new son, Josh; and my father was now retired and loved working with our horses and doing the gardening on our acreage while my mother enjoyed caring for our guest house in which they now lived.

Jinger's eventual first pregnancy was a difficult one and I suspended my MORE THAN FRIENDS activities until the baby was born. In the following months, little B.J. captured our hearts with his infectious laughter and gentle, loving spirit. Being with him became a special time of peace for me as I resumed my whirlwind activities with MORE THAN FRIENDS.

Finding and training coordinators for the new groups took most of my time and energy. As I poured myself into the new group leaders, I leaned on Kay more and more. Kay resented the pressure, but I felt I had no one else to turn to. When the tension between us became intolerable, Kay decided to go to Burlingame, California, for two weeks of intensive therapy with Dr. Osborne, the man whose book had set us both on this path.

Dr. Osborne's counseling center specialized in regressive therapy. He believed that uncovering childhood deprivation and trauma helped many people deal with present day difficulties. Kay felt that spending some time with Dr. Osborne would help her with her personal problems and perhaps with our conflicts.

Kay returned from California with a clearer

sense of herself and began to place limits on my time with her. While I was happy for her growth as a person, her pulling away hurt me deeply. Kay's withdrawal made me feel as though my whole foundation was collapsing.

Kay encouraged me to go to Burlingame. She often said, "Marilyn, you are the most driven person I know. You accomplish so much, but it's killing you." And she insisted, "There must have been something in your childhood to make you react this way." I vehemently denied that I needed therapy and countered with, "You had a painful childhood, Kay, and you know it. But I don't need therapy. I had a perfect childhood."

While Kay was setting healthy boundaries with me, I continued to bury myself deeper into our exploding concept of MORE THAN FRIENDS. We now had thirty-five groups in the Phoenix area and new groups starting in three other states. Along with training coordinators, I prepared monthly newsletters, searched for new study material, and wrote workbooks. I arranged special functions involving all the group members, while creating new groups out of the growing stack of registration cards.

For several years, I thought of MORE THAN FRIENDS as a snowball cascading down a hill at breakneck speed. But now it was becoming like the white mass in my childhood nightmares, suddenly turning into an avalanche and burying me beneath it. I felt overwhelmed by the responsibility, by the sense that everyone depended on me. I was afraid the whole organization would fall apart if I did not keep on top of everything. I was afraid to let go, but afraid, also, that I could not withstand the pressure.

"Dear God," I would plead, "I'm not sure I can handle this. It's so much more than I ever expected. I want to 'kiss it and make it well' for everyone and I can't!"

As MORE THAN FRIENDS grew, so did my physical pain. My daily dosage of medication was now 25 tablets of Excedrin, 125 milligrams of Elavil, and 8 to 10 tablets of Alka-Seltzer, plus a bottle of Fiornal a week—with almost no effect. Sometimes my pain was so great I would spend days in bed. But even there, my work followed me. I dictated training manuals and letters from my bed, determined to get all the information down on paper before I died. I wanted to die. If I died, there would be no more pain.

One night, as I started to slip away into welcome sleep, a savage pain pierced my chest. It gained intensity so rapidly that I could hardly breathe. I gasped as the feeling raced through my veins, muscles, joints, every cell, until it permeated my body. A terrifying sound filled my ears. It began deep and low, escalating in pitch until I felt I would explode. It became a wail, an inner scream. As it reached glass-shattering decibels, the pain in my chest swelled until I felt my heart would burst.

My breath was caught in my lungs, held in anticipation of being released in one final, catastrophic explosion. I begged, "Please God, just let me die." The piercing pain slowly subsided. Instead of feeling relieved, I felt frustrated.

The following evening, Todd came home from work to find me writhing on the bed. The intensity of the explosions in my head made me nearly hysterical. He immediately took me to the hospital.

The doctor administered a massive dose of Demerol, but the pain persisted.

On September 18, 1980, my MORE THAN FRIENDS group arranged a birthday dinner party for me at one of the women's homes. It was also an intervention. These friends gave me a strong dose of tough love as they pointed out areas of my life that showed I had problems other than physical ones.

"Marilyn, are you even vaguely aware of some of our reactions to your excessive perfectionism and altruism? We feel inferior because we can't ever return enough in kind to you. You're so busy giving and doing that we feel inadequate. You're setting standards so high that we couldn't begin to meet them. It makes us uncomfortable—and it's killing you."

The pounding in my skull became a deafening roar. I burned hot, then icy cold. I struggled to keep the tears from engulfing me as my friends continued. "You've become obsessed with 'caring'—caring for others, but not for yourself. We feel you definitely need to see a qualified counselor—*NOW*."

I left the "party" and drove home alone. I was stunned, angry, and hurt. I knew that Kay had felt these things, but I had no idea the others felt the same way. As I drove home, I made a plan. My first step would be to end all the medication I had been taking. While I had always been ready to recommend counseling to other people, I still felt therapy was not an option for me. Suicide seemed the only remaining choice. I had always been taught that Christians cannot commit suicide. Now I began to believe that might not be true.

Pain is a great leveler, a great humbler. Pain knocks you down and stomps on you. When you struggle to your feet, it knocks you down and stomps on you again. Excruciating pain, physical or emotional, pain from which you cannot escape, strips you of all reason. It short-circuits the brain.

I contemplated ways in which I could take my life so it would look accidental. Maintaining my image had become more important than maintaining my life. My first task was to prepare for my family. I took Missy through the house and showed her the lists of household items and their value: paintings, china, silver, photographs, tax records. Missy listened patiently at first, then she pulled back. "Mother, this is morbid."

At eight o'clock one evening I received a call from Kay. I was already in bed and in tears from intense pain. When Kay heard my quivering voice, she did not try to hide her indignation. "Where the hell is Todd, anyway? He should be taking care of you."

Wearily I replied, "Todd can't face my pain. What can he do anyway? Nothing works anymore."

"Well, something's got to be done. You have to get help. I will not let you die."

"Kay," I whispered, "What can I do? I've tried everything."

"I insist you go to Burlingame for therapy. I'll call Dr. Osborne and see if I can get you in immediately."

"But," I argued, "I have so much work to do with MORE THAN FRIENDS. Besides, Todd will never agree to it."

"You leave Todd to me," Kay responded. "MORE THAN FRIENDS has plenty of women able to take your responsibilities. I'm going to call the airlines first thing in the morning and make your reservation."

"Marilyn," she finished, "You no longer have any choice!"

Part Two

Releasing the Sobbing Hurting Child

*Myself, Missy, and Jinger, on Thanksgiving, 1980,
just three days before I left for therapy.*

♦ 5 ♦

The Volcano

Thanksgiving weekend, 1980.

I hardly noticed the turbulence of the plane as it flew over the unstable desert air. I had my briefcase open on my tray table, sorting through the work that needed to be done. Try as I might, my mind would not focus on the work at hand.

Kay, true to her word, had made all arrangements and had even driven me to the airport. Still struggling with disbelief in my need for therapy or in its effectiveness for me, I had boarded the plane for California—another frontier.

Inside the San Francisco airport terminal, a young man approached me. "Hi, you must be Marilyn. I'm Jerry. Babette asked me to come get you." Babette Baker housed many of Dr. Osborne's out-of-town clients.

As we drove the few miles to Burlingame, Jerry told me how the therapy he received changed his life. I hid my skepticism behind a smile. When we turned off the freeway, I commented, "This place reminds me of Kansas—the wet, cold weather and the large old houses with hedges in front. Look, the trees arch across the street just like home."

Jerry turned in the driveway of a beautiful two-story home with a well-manicured front lawn. A small woman with a cheerful smile greeted us. "Kay's been telling me all about you," Babette bubbled. "I thought I'd give you the room she stayed in. It's back here."

I followed her through the hallway to a charming bedroom at the back of the house. Twin beds snuggled up against a bright floral wallpaper. I unpacked, thinking this would be a comfortable place for my two-week stay, then sat in the living room with Babette and talked about Dr. Osborne and the center.

I learned that Babette had worked with Dr. Osborne for twenty-three years and was now assistant director at his counseling center. Later, her husband Don joined us and introduced himself with a good natured greeting. I was amazed that he was so supportive of her work. My admiration continued to grow as I found their house to be occupied not only by Jerry and me, but by several other clients from the center.

That evening, I felt cold and tired from the trip. I climbed into bed early and turned my electric blanket on high. My thoughts tumbled in doubt and confusion. I wanted only two things: to be released from my excruciating pain and to be in God's will for the rest of my life. I was not at all certain that the latter meant that I should be here.

My first appointment at the center was with Dr. Osborne. He was a comfortable friend, having been to Phoenix several times for MORE THAN FRIENDS functions. He described the purposes of regressive therapy. "Children are often encouraged to express their positive, loving feelings, but are discouraged in expressing anything negative."

Dr. Osborne explained that these negative, hurtful feelings that the child buries create problems, both psychological and physiological, as the child grows into an adult. "The purpose of this type of therapy is to allow those buried, painful memories to surface."

I forced a smile, crossed my legs, and tried to concentrate on Dr. Osborne's words as he continued. "Marilyn, we all have a 'pool of pain.' As products of our environment, none of us is the totally unblemished child we were created to be."

"But," I protested, "I really don't need this type of therapy. I am one of the few people that had a perfect childhood. My parents genuinely loved me."

He smiled gently and said, "Many people who come here feel that way. It's not uncommon to have only a few painful memories. People come for therapy for many reasons. Not everyone has obvious emotional problems. Some come because they have difficulties in their relationships, or, like you, because of severe physical pain."

I asked what happens in a therapy session.

"You'll feel as though you're on a split screen. Your adult stands off to one side, totally conscious of all that's happening. As your inner child is released, your voice will start to sound like a child's, not like an adult's."

I moved uneasily in my chair. "That sounds strange." Dr. Osborne agreed. "It is a strange feeling at first. You will work with one of four therapists."

He paused a moment, then stood. "Let's go upstairs to the therapy room."

As I entered, I glanced around the room. The room was almost empty. There was a large mat in the center, and off to the side, a few big, brightly colored pillows lay near a tape player. Background music, to encourage relaxation, played quietly. A night light provided the only light for the windowless room.

I felt awkward and foolish as I lay down on the mat. Dr. Osborne sat near my head, asking me to breathe deeply. "Let your thoughts and your feelings flow freely. Be conscious of any thought or visual concept that surfaces and verbalize it to me."

Stiff and unyielding, I talked softly to myself, trying to allow my feelings to emerge. Finally I sat up. "I can never do this! This seems so unorthodox and weird. I want to leave right now."

He touched my shoulder. "Don't be so hard on yourself. You just need a little more time."

"I can't turn off my mind. It races."

On Monday and Tuesday I talked to the therapists and tried to allow myself to relax. My thoughts continually returned to my volatile friendship with Kay and my eyes flooded with tears at the remembrance of Ginger.

"Ginger was the only friend I had who loved me as much as I loved her. Maybe more. She had the strength to write that letter, and I didn't even answer it."

I closed my eyes, thinking through every detail of the past. "We had so much fun together. Crazy Ginger. She did everything I wanted to do but didn't." The tears started again. "I couldn't go to her funeral. I feel I failed her. Sometimes it's hard for me to realize she's gone."

Gradually I began to accept that Ginger was dead, and I could not replace her with Kay. Despite this new understanding, my small insights frustrated me. I felt as if I tapped only the surface of my problems. On the other hand, I did not think there was really anything significant to uncover.

Wednesday evening when I left the center, there was a cold, drizzling rain. The dampness and darkness reached inside me, touching something black and cold. It was as if something or someone I did not know lived inside me and peered out through my eyes. The familiar return walk to Babette's became a journey through Alice's Wonderland: the route became longer and less familiar and I seemed to grow smaller. The many hedges along the sidewalk stood as a barrier against something terrifying.

I swallowed hard, my stomach turning over and over, warning me of some unseen danger behind the hedges. "I feel so foolish," I muttered to myself. "Can't walk on the sidewalks. Like some crazy person afraid of the dark. I hope no one catches me walking in the street."

I looked around furtively. *It's so different from the Arizona desert,* I thought. The houses and naked trees looked more and more like Kansas. I shivered and then rounded the corner, glad to see the warmth and security of Babette's house ahead of me.

Thursday morning dawned as miserable as I felt. The grey drizzling rain seeped inside me, settling like a heavy weight in my chest. I turned my mind away from the frustrations of not getting anywhere with my therapy and concentrated on the slide presentation I planned to give at lunch: pictures and words over a background of quiet music, telling the story of MORE THAN FRIENDS. Dr. Osborne and his book were mentioned in it, so he wanted to see what had been said about him. I was anxious to hear his response.

The staff and several clients crowded into the room to watch. I had seen the presentation only once before. This time I paid less attention to the words and more attention to the pictures. I pointed out Kay as an adorable youngster with a very sad face. Then an eight-year-old Marilyn, clutching a doll, stood in front of a big old house in Wichita. I watched, gulped, and then the image was gone. *What was that feeling of fear and foreboding that raced through me?* I shuddered and then pulled myself out in time to chuckle with the others over the photo taken my senior year in high school.

As I walked home from the center more slowly than usual, the weight in my chest grew thicker and started to rattle with my old antagonist, asthma. Chills shook my body and my temperature rose to 102 degrees.

Wheezing and choking, I continued therapy on Friday. A weekend of rest did not ease my distress. I wanted to go home to Arizona, perhaps even to the hospital.

On Monday I felt no better. Lying flat on the mat only made the coughing worse, so the therapist propped me up on a pillow.

"I'm sorry I'm so sick," I said hoarsely. "I haven't had an asthma attack in about twenty-five

This is the photo I saw on the slide presentation.
I am eight years old and in front of the big
old white house in Wichita.

years, not since I was in the hospital on oxygen after my wedding."

"Close your eyes and let yourself drift back to your first experience with asthma," the therapist suggested.

To my great surprise, I soon felt as though I was actually in that first attack. "I'm eight," I explained. "I'm begging my mother to stay with me because every time I try to go to sleep I have a horrible nightmare."

Then I heard a small, unfamiliar voice say, "I hate the dream—hate the dream—it scares me so."

My conscious mind had not willed those words. The words came completely unbidden. The voice that spoke them was of a small child, not my adult voice. Amazement and fear swept over me, but also a sense of intrigue and curiosity. *What else could this child possibly have to tell me?*

The session continued. My memories flashed forward to the first summer after the original asthma attack, forward to the missed summer camp, and then to the senior sneak trip. "I hate being sick. I don't want to be different. I want to do everything like the other kids!" I moaned slightly, my voice getting softer. "My head hurts."

I sat up, surprised at how quickly things began to make sense. I immediately started making connections. "I never thought of myself as a sickly kid. I guess I blocked out how much it really bothered me."

The session revealed a pattern. Throughout my life, in various situations, I felt responsible for taking care of myself—through my mother's migraines, during the war, in medicating myself for my asthma, and by being the only person who could breathe for me.

Now I knew that my child had decided unconsciously to be the best intellectually. It was my only option because I could not compete physically. As a child and as an adult, I had never wanted to play a game I could not win.

I was excited about this insight. "Now I understand why I'm so driven. It's all the result of my asthma." Then I added rather confidently, "I think I'm ready to go home now, don't you?"

The therapist smiled. "I think you better stay just a bit longer."

In my next session, more new thoughts emerged. "When I was eight, I decided to be something other than what I was. So I started to imitate others . . .," my voice drifted, like a small boat needing direction.

A soft voice gave me that direction.

"Describe all the houses in which you lived as a child. Tell me about each one, whether it was a good house or a bad house."

Propped up to breathe, I began reciting the houses. I could remember the wallpaper, the design, the size. I cheerily described each as a "good" house. My mind suddenly whirled and flashed to the house in Wichita, the house I had seen on the slide in the MORE THAN FRIENDS presentation. "It's a *bad* house," a guttural voice said.

"Why?"

Shifting gears, I spoke in my normal adult voice. "I think it's because that's where I first became sick with asthma. One afternoon a week, I took the bus to choir practice and one afternoon I went to piano

lessons after school and walked home in the dark,"
I explained.

"I know it was dark because in the winter it gets
dark at five o'clock. In those days everyone listened
to the Lone Ranger, and he came on at six. I used to
hear the William Tell Overture being played from
house to house as I hurried along, trying to get
home before the program was over.

"I wondered in later years why I was allowed to
walk home in the dark, but my mother replied it
was common in those days. Unlike today, nothing
bad ever happened to anyone then."

I then proceeded to describe the next house.

By Tuesday, December 9, 1980, my asthma and
exhaustion were gradually destroying my physical
and emotional defenses. In my therapy sessions, I
immediately dropped back to my childhood
asthma attacks. Often coughing and choking, my
breathing continued to be difficult. In one particular session, I lay on the mat with my eyes closed.
Sensing movement over the top of me, I opened my
eyes in time to see a pillow coming down slowly
onto my face.

Silently I said, *What in the world are you doing!
You know how scared I am of being smothered. If
you touch me with that pillow I'll kick you clear
across the room!*

The pillow touched my face. To my astonishment my labored breathing became shallow, so
shallow I felt as if I had died.

Dead.

Nothing matters anymore. I am dead.

The therapist gently shook my shoulder. "Marilyn, Marilyn, what's happening?"

The Volcano

A strange voice rose from some shadowy darkness deep inside me, "I died."

The therapist began to remove the pillow from my face, but I reached up and pulled it back down. *I want to stay dead.* Something was wrong. Terribly wrong.

He placed a longer pillow lengthwise over my body.

A peaceful smile touched my lips. *A casket surrounds me. A smooth, cool satin lining cradles my body.*

My hand touched my face, and I started to cry.

"What's wrong?" the therapist asked softly.

"There's a lady touching my face at my funeral. She's sad because I'm dead. I feel bad that I'm making her cry."

Suddenly it is dark and very still. *I'm buried deep in my grave.* A voice no more than a whisper manages to say, "It's peaceful and quiet. No more crying. I like it here. I want to stay."

A hurricane blew through my mind, disheveling my thoughts. I was suffocated by the feeling that I was not only dead, but that I did not exist. I always thought death meant being "absent from the body and at home with the Lord." Now death meant cessation of existence. Now I was nowhere. Not in heaven. Not in hell. Nowhere. I did not exist.

The therapist lifted the pillow. The session had ended, but not inside me. I was grateful for the two-hour wait before the evening's group session began.

After hearing about my afternoon's experience, another therapist directed me into her therapy room. I lay on the mat, and she pulled a sheet over my head. Immediately I was dead again, buried in a

But – much to my great surprise & now my utter confusion – I welcomed it!! I did not fight it – I cannot say the feeling – there are no words. I stopped breathing – my heart stopped beating, I was so still – I died. For a long time I remained that way – I was aware of the sounds in the next room – of Pete shaking my shoulder & calling my name – but wanting to remain dead! Pete kept asking "what's happening?" I finally gave a muffled sob (my hand was over my mouth) & said "I died" He removed the pillow & I reached up & pulled it back down over me – I wanted to remain dead! I stayed totally unmoving for what seemed like a very long time – with my breathing so small as to be totally unnoticeable. (How could I do that when for days & nights I haven't been able to take one unlabored breath!?)

My journal after I experienced my "death" session, written about 5:30 p.m. on Tuesday night.

box. Her soft voice encouraged, "Why don't you let the 'real Marilyn' come out and talk to me?"

A child's small voice replied, "No, she's dead. She can't talk. She doesn't have a voice. She can't talk."

Small hands touched my face, trembling, walking as if they were little people exploring a new land. The hands touched each other, unfamiliar. The small voice took on a new intensity, filled with disbelief and confusion. "But these aren't my hands, and this isn't my face."

The music in the player shifted, marching across the room, whipping a new fear into me. "Oh, ohh, soldiers! I can see their boots and their uniforms. They're marching over my grave! But I won't feel any pain and I won't be scared, because they don't know I'm here. I'm buried so deep. And even if they could find me, they couldn't hurt me because I don't have any feelings anymore. I'm dead."

The music crashed, and the little voice rose in terror. "It's wartime! It's wartime! The bombs are falling! Look! One of them just blew the dirt off my grave!" My body felt as though it were rising into the air, blown out of the ground.

"I'm on top of the ground now. Look. The bomb has burned everything. There are no more flowers." My hands patted the mat around me. "The ground is black and dirty, the trees have no leaves." I paused a moment, the terror eased by a new thought. "I'm all alone now. The soldiers are gone."

Then, far off in the distance, I saw them again. "They're looking at me and laughing. They aren't people. They have Martian faces with big buggy eyes!"

I stared at the sheet, my voice returning to normal, pleading with the therapist. "My Lord, what's happening to me?"

She shut off the music and pulled the sheet off me. "Marilyn, something *did* happen to you in your childhood. But our time is up. We have to stop now."

"Stop? How can I stop? Something is rolling, and I don't even know what it is!"

"You need to allow yourself to find out what it is. Go sit in Dr. Osborne's office and write down anything that comes to you. Try to see if you can discover something more."

I felt confused, scared, dazed, my body limp and weighted at the same time. Walking to Dr. Osborne's office was nearly impossible. When I got there, I did not bother to turn on the lights. Two large Arcadia doors allowed enough illumination from the street light and passing cars for me to see.

I sat on the couch, pushed off my shoes, and lay down, wishing I could drop further into the couch's leathery folds to hide myself from the truth. I knew that some of the women who came to see Dr. Osborne discovered they were victims of incest. *Please, dear God, please don't let that be me.*

My hands gripped the sofa cushion on each side. I swallowed hard and began the process of sorting through every male member of my family. With relief, I realized none of them had ever done anything to hurt me. I closed my eyes, naming all the boys I had ever dated. Nothing.

But the fear did not leave. It grew. From a tangled

mass containing years of memories, oozing up from a dark pit, the voice of a terrified little girl stammered, "That house, that house. That bad house! It's wartime. Soldiers, soldiers, that bad house! Oh! Ohh!"

Suddenly it erupted. A volcano, after years of festering and rumbling, burst forth as an inhuman sound, splitting the air. Stark, screaming, naked terror. It spewed out, strangling me. My mind exploded violently, rending, tearing, shredding.

My God, my God. It happened to me.

It happened to me then, and it's happening to me now! Oh, dear God, please don't let this happen to me! *NO. NO. NOT ME!*

In the darkness I felt brutal arms slam around my chest in a sudden clamp. Giant hands seized me, twisting my arm behind my back. "Please, please, you're hurting my arm!"

Unseen forces violently snatched up my body and threw it off the couch and over the coffee table. *What's happening? What's happening to me?!!*

My body was consumed by memories bursting forth with uncontrolled ferocity. I doubled over as a remembered kick connected with my stomach. I reeled and fell. Struggling to get to my knees, I was kicked again. *Can't get away. Can't escape the boots, the blows to my body.*

"I'm only eight. I'm only eight! Please, please, I'm such a little girl. Won't somebody please help me? I'm so little!"

A scream from both a child and a woman:

"Won't someone please help me?"

♦ 6 ♦

A Box of Crayons

My screams brought others running. One man raced to get a therapist for help.

Far away, I heard a soft voice. "It's Pete. I'm here." His hand gently touched me. His touch felt so different from the pain I had just experienced, but in the next moment, I was off again, tumbling and crashing about the room.

The torment continued for several hours as my body released its horrifying secret. Back and forth I whipped across the room—under the desk, into the corners, over the chairs.

It all came back, nearly all of it. Eight years old with my nose in a book, I had missed my bus stop going home from choir practice or my piano lesson. Getting off in a strange part of town, I walked, trying to get back to where I belonged.

From behind a dark hedge, massive arms grabbed me suddenly and violently, like steel bands encircling my chest. Soldiers, lots of soldiers, laughed and jeered, playing an ugly game. I was thrown, tossed, dropped. Boots gave a playful kick into a cringing side.

Hysterical screams splattered the air. "I'm so

little! Won't somebody please help me? I'm only eight! I'm only eight!" A tiny voice pleaded frantically, "Please, please, you're hurting my arm. Please don't hurt me anymore."

I can't get up. I can't get away. I can't run fast enough.

I staggered and fell. Another kick. *They think this is fun. I'm so scared and they think this is a game!*

A blur of lights, arms, legs, and uniforms confused my mind. Cowering on my knees, spinning in a tight little circle, I reached out, touching the shiny toes of their shoes. "One, two, three, four, five, six, seven, eight, nine . . ."

Whimpering, like a wounded rabbit against a pack of wolves, the little girl trembled.

Brutal hands held my arms and legs, while others peeled away my clothes, tossing them on the nearby hedge.

"Stop, please stop. What are you doing?" the hysterical voice pleaded.

A street light on the empty lot reflected in the shiny buttons and medals decorating the massive figures looming over me. Four of them grabbed each of my hands and feet, staking me out into a pitiful naked X. Heavy forms sat on my legs, pressing them into the icy ground.

Suddenly, I was no longer a part of the violence. I was high up in a tree, looking down on the horrible scene. The men, standing in a circle, laughed and mocked that pathetic little girl, so white and naked against the black frozen ground.

The soldiers violently yanked my head backward, and I saw the trees where I perched just a split second before. *The trees have no leaves,* I thought, almost as if they, too, betrayed me. Cruel fingers pulled at my hair, trying to keep my wildly thrashing head from moving. "Hold still little girl, or you'll really get hurt."

Something repulsive pressed onto my face, covering it completely.

"I can't breathe! I can't breathe!"

They forced my mouth open. A huge object rushed in, spewing a vile tasting substance down my throat. My muscles constricted in uncontrolled gagging and choking. I tried to spit it out.

I'm dying. Oh God, help me. Don't let me die. I'm so afraid. Please, please God. Don't walk away from me.

The lights from the passing cars tormented me. Cars filled with people. People who will not listen to my screams and don't care enough to come help. *I'm such a bad girl. If I was a good girl, someone would surely come help me.*

Frenzied shouts incited the next attacker. They twisted the little eight-year-old body into grotesque contortions. Nausea rushed over me in unending waves.

Dear God, just let me die! I can't stand this. I'm choking to death. It hurts so bad. I'm too tired to fight. I can't move and I can't scream anymore.

Then, with one last burst of energy, a final effort at survival, I fought back and was knocked unconscious. Peaceful blackness swept over me.

Minutes seemed like hours. I woke to silence. Slowly, slowly my head began to move.

With my face pressed against the mat, my voice was barely audible. "I am dead. I am dead. No more soldiers. No more pain, no more terror, no more screaming. Nothing but peace and rest. If I crawl under this bush, I'll die. I'm naked and so cold."

Another, new voice began to speak. "You've got to go home. Your mommy and daddy will be worried about you."

The small voice reproached, "I'm already dead. I don't have any feelings anymore. Leave me alone. Can't you see I'm dead?"

Minutes later, a chilling cold and a strong need to find my shoes consumed me. "I have to get up and go home."

Frantically I searched for my shoes. Totally exhausted and caught in painful memories, I dragged myself by my fingers, inch by inch, back and forth across the dark room, looking in vain for my shoes.

Why doesn't anyone come and help me? It must be because I'm so dirty and ugly that they can't bear to look at me. I don't want them to come and find me now. I can't have anyone see me looking like this. I'm bad, so bad. I'm so tired. I can't go home now. If I go home without my shoes my mother will know I've been bad. I can't ever tell anyone what happened. It will make my mommy cry and my daddy mad. I want only to die. I deserve to die. I'm so bad.

The huge office desk changed into a hedge. Inch by inch I crawled under it. *I've got to hide so no one can find me.*

Strange fingers, attached to my hand, lightly touched my face. *Weeping. Someone is weeping. Not an actual woman. But a female being. She's the same lady who cried at my funeral this afternoon. She's bigger and stronger than me, but she's not a mommy. She won't say, "Bad, bad." She'll take care of me.*

I stroked my face, while the female being talked to my abused child. "Poor, poor baby. Just look what they've done to you! You've lost your shoes. You've got to find your shoes and get up and go home. Your mommy and daddy will worry about you. You've got to go home."

Why doesn't she leave me alone! She knows I'm dead.

An incredible thing began to happen. No longer in my body, I stood off to one side. It was as if I were now three distinct persons: an observing woman, a protective female being, and an eight-year-old child.

I watched the female being go over to my lifeless child-form and pick up only my head, because that's what held all my feelings. The choice had been made: to kill the essence of Marilyn Reh, the core of my being. A terrible decision, but it had to be made: bury the child so the body could go on living.

Putting my head into a small metal box, the female being walked across the empty lot to where the attack took place.

She put the box into a hole in the ground and piled dirt and rocks on it, burying it. "There, there baby. Nobody will ever hurt you again. You'll never feel again. I'm digging your grave so deep that the soldiers can march over your grave, and they won't be able to see you. But even if they could find you, they can't ever, ever hurt you again, because you're dead. I'll bury all of your feelings down deep. Just remember to stay dead and never ever feel again. To feel hurts. I'll never let you hurt again, not ever!"

I pounded the office floor over and over, pounding the dirt on that little grave, burying the sobbing, hurting child.

Finally, my mind shifted and split. I became the sobbing, hurting child in my grave. "I like it here in my box, in my grave. It's quiet and comfortable," my child insisted. "So peaceful. No more pain. No crying, no terror."

The little child looked up from my grave and saw the female being searching for my shoes. In a few seconds, she walked to the grave, shoes in hand.

"Look. She's taking my clothes off the hedge and now she's putting them on my body. She's washing my face and hands with snow. She's smoothing down my hair and putting my cap on my head. Now she's crawling into my empty body! *My* body with *my* shoes on *my* feet are walking over the top of this grave."

The strange female being paused and straightened up the small child's body. Then, slowly, deliberately, she raised my hands to my face, stroked it from the corners of my mouth up my cheeks and put a smile on my face, a smile that would become a permanent mask for the next thirty-six years, a death mask covering an ancient tomb.

She's leaving me!

In the quiet darkness of the grave, the eight-year-old settled down into the box. But the peace was gone.

I've been a bad girl tonight. I guess I'm not bad enough to go to hell. But now I'm not good enough to go to heaven. I must be very bad, because even God didn't want to send anyone to help me. I was so dirty and guilty even He couldn't bear to look at me. He just turned and looked the other way.

The child thought a little more. *He's saying the kindest thing that He can do for me is to erase me. He simply took His giant hand and wiped it across me like an eraser on a school blackboard. He just erased me! I don't exist. No more emotions and no soul.*

I shook my head, tears pouring down my face, sobs choking me. "This can't be. It can't be! No one could possibly bury such a horrendous trauma. I have to be imagining this. My memory has always been a source of pride to me. I could never forget anything of this magnitude."

Words and tears poured out together. The therapist, Dr. Peter Danylchuk, listened. He did not suggest or push. He let the memories speak to me. I had had enough trauma for one night. He would not make it worse.

At about midnight, Dr. Danylchuk helped me to his car and drove me back to Babette's.

Babette, accustomed to caring for many deeply hurting persons, lovingly helped me into bed. The instant my head touched the pillow, unwanted screams poured forth. Terror rolled again in full force. My fingernails clawed the sheets, ripping, tearing, frantically trying to get away. Babette lay on top of me to keep me from destroying the room. After several hours, my thrashing and screaming slowed to an agitated whimpering. My voice, soft and breathless, suggested Babette sleep in the other bed. "I might be okay as long as you leave the lights on."

As Babette slept, I sat bolt upright in bed. *Dear God! Did this really happen to me!*

As the day dawned, a new plea poured out from me. "Lord, please don't let this have happened to me. Give me one thing I can hold in my hand so I can be certain."

My trembling hand reached for my journal to express the overwhelming feelings still pouring through me. I closed my eyes, my hand moving slowly across the page. I opened my eyes to read the childish scrawl: "I can't write. I'm only 8." The pen clattered to the floor, my hand and my heart leaping to my throat.

"It can't be true," I moaned through fresh tears. "Am I really only eight? I have a husband, family, MORE THAN FRIENDS, so many people who count on me! Please Lord, surely you're not going to leave me as an eight year-old?"

With a trembling hand, I leaned over to pick up the pen again. With great effort and determination I wrote the alphabet in big loopy circles. The experience was new and fresh, as awkward as learning to write cursive in the third grade. Reaching the letter "M", I felt that I should write my name. *MARILYN* looked big and loopy too. But then, what about a last name? Confusion whirled inside me. "I don't have a last name. Marilyn *Murray* doesn't exist yet, and Marilyn *Reh* is dead."

I started to write "*Reh*," but my hand fell, dragging the pen down the page. *I don't exist. I don't exist.* The pen lay in my lap as I put my hands over my face, stunned by the reality thrust in front of me.

I both looked forward to and feared my therapy sessions for that day. I feared the truth emerging before my disbelieving conscious self, yet I looked forward to the purging of the ugliness hidden inside me for so many years.

The session was seven hours long. The vileness of the soldiers' attack poured forth with an intensity I could not have foreseen. I was left reeling, shocked and exhausted, and I was frightened by the realization that now three totally different "Marilyns" existed. When I tried to explain this split to Dr. Danylchuk, I struggled to find the right words, mixing the thoughts and feelings of an adult and an eight year-old.

"I feel as if when I was created, I was an Original Feeling Child. When the attack happened, I turned into a Sobbing Hurting Child. Then, in order to stay alive, I became a Controlling Child. She buried the other two and said, 'Never feel again!' Then she took my body home and eventually grew up to be the 'big Marilyn,' the lady who brought me here.

"My Controlling Child wasn't 'born.' She came only to help me, to protect me. My Original Feeling Child, who was born into my body, disappeared when I felt that God erased my soul. She was buried along with my Sobbing Child. But now, for the first time in thirty-six years, my Original Feeling Child has my body back again!"

That evening, my Original Feeling Child was adamant as she talked to Babette. "I don't want to give my body back to the big Marilyn! I know she kept me alive during the attack. Because of her, I've had a happy life, never remembering or knowing about that hideous event, never being afraid of men, soldiers, or the dark. But I'm kind of mad at the big Marilyn. I wanted to die. It would have been so much easier, and she wouldn't let me!" My lips puckered with little-girl indignation.

"At last I have my very own body back, and I intend to keep it. It's mine. I was born with it, and I won't let her have it!" My arms patted and hugged my body with enthusiasm.

My adult Marilyn seemed quite surprised at the emergence of this tough, stubborn little kid. I had always seen myself as agreeable and compliant. I began to recognize the roots of my continual need for control.

Thursday morning I awoke anxious to get to the center and see Dr. Danylchuk. The painful memories never seemed to quit. To avoid them, I reached over, picked up my journal and practiced writing the alphabet. As Babette walked by the kitchen table, I said, "I'm doing my homework to take to Dr. Danylchuk. It feels like he's my teacher."

Later, during my session, I asked him, "Is it okay to just stay just eight? It's really hard to be big right now."

"Yes, it's okay," he reassured me.

But even with his supportive comments, I flipped back into the "big Marilyn." I was worried about my family.

"Have you told them yet? No one will possibly understand. It'll be devastating to them."

Dr. Danylchuk answered, "I called your husband today."

I felt frantic. "I'm supposed to go home Saturday,

but how can I? But I have to. It's my grandson B.J.'s first birthday. I have house guests arriving from out of town on Sunday. Then I'm having an open house for more than a hundred people, and invitations have already been sent out for a sit-down dinner party for seventy people the week before Christmas."

Dr. Danylchuk leaned over his pad of paper to touch my shoulder. "I'll take care of it. You're going to need all your strength and resources just to take care of yourself."

"But what about Christmas?" I wailed. "How can I ruin Christmas for everyone? I don't think my eight-year-old can handle all of this."

"Don't worry about any of it. Now it's your turn to sit back and let others take care of you."

Within a week, unusual occurrences started to take place. My appetite changed. I no longer wanted the artichoke I bought the day I arrived. Instead, I preferred my childhood favorites of milk, crackers, peanut butter, and honey. With the appetite change came a weight loss. My shape changed from being small waisted with large hips to become wider in my waist, more square and child-like. Even the hair under my arms and on my legs stopped growing.

I could not tolerate wearing a bra and refused to bother with make-up or jewelry. The thought of driving a car put me into a panic, so Babette drove me anywhere I needed to go. Always self-sufficient and taking care of everyone, I hated to be in the position where I needed to rely on others to take care of me, but the little girl inside of me insisted on being "just eight," no matter how inconvenient.

A Box of Crayons

Cautiously, I ventured to Babette, "I really would like something to do."

"How about going to a toy store?" Babette offered.

At the store, I looked at all the things I could choose. "I like these coloring books and this big box of crayons. I'll get a penmanship book so I can practice my writing and a math book. I really need help on that."

"Would you like some books to read, too?" Babette asked.

"Oh, yes! I love to read."

Babette drove to the library and chose some books for me from the young readers section.

Before long, a routine was established. Still afraid to walk the one-half mile to the center alone, I rode with Babette when she went to work at eight and came home with her at five. I spent four or more hours a day in therapy sessions. The rest of the time, I sat in the kitchenette coloring or doing my "homework."

For a few days I was self-conscious about being a forty-four-year-old woman carrying a coloring book and a third-grade reader instead of a briefcase. Occasionally, some of the other clients came into the kitchenette to sit and color with me or to hold me when I was in tears and afraid. Gradually I began to feel more comfortable about my eight-year-old child inside an adult body.

Almost without ceasing, I prayed, "Dear Lord, did this actually happen to me? Please give me something to prove that this is real."

It was as though my life were a giant puzzle that had been dumped upside down in a jumbled heap.

Each day I would turn a few pieces over and try to make them fit. Sometimes a piece of sky, then a tree, a snatch of dirt. It all seemed so terribly confused.

One day, I remembered a visit to a doctor earlier in the year. The doctor, attempting to discover the reasons for my headaches, x-rayed my head. He showed me a spot at the base of my skull, asking me how I received the concussion there.

I replied, "But I've never had a concussion."

"Anyone who was hit hard enough to have this type of injury has got to be able to remember it. You must have fallen, or you were in an accident."

"I have an excellent memory. Nothing like that ever happened to me," I protested.

I told Dr. Danylchuk about the x-ray. "The spot on the x-ray is exactly the point where the man struck me unconscious. How ironic. It probably saved my life. Maybe the men thought they had killed me and then left me for dead."

Dr. Danylchuk agreed with me. "Can you remember what that little girl did to get home. What did you tell your parents?"

In my next session, I allowed my Controlling Child to take over. I watched her crawl into my body, again putting on the smile mask. "I walk home, tell my mother I was reading on the bus and missed my stop. I play a few moments with my baby sister and then go upstairs to bathe. I bathe myself and put on my long flannel pajamas."

My adult added more insights. "It was an oral rape, and oral rape leaves no cuts, tears, or bleeding. Fortunately I had on a heavy snow suit that protected me during the first part of the attack, when I was being kicked and thrown into the snow banks. Later, after my clothes were peeled off, I was held down so tightly that I couldn't fight. You get hurt the most when you're struggling and fighting back. And I couldn't do that."

Dr. Danylchuk reached over and touched my arm. "Slow down a bit. It'll all make sense eventually."

"I probably did have some bruises, but no one would ever see them under the long-sleeved sweaters and pants or long stockings that I wore every day in the winter, would they? And all kids get some bruises playing."

Dr. Danylchuk nodded as he spoke, "It sounds reasonable. But I've been wondering if there weren't some changes in your personality."

"I'm sure there were. But any changes could have been attributed to so many things. I was an only child for eight years, and then my mother had a new baby just before we moved to Wichita. We moved three times in nine months, and I changed schools each time. I had to make all new friends and get used to new teachers. Then, of course, I started to have asthma and missed a lot of school. And don't forget my nightmares."

Dr. Danylchuk commented, "When you were growing up, most people did not think about what caused nightmares, and people certainly did not consider possible abuse. Your mother probably did not have the slightest idea about what had happened to you."

Every day in therapy I relived the terror of the attack, and each time the events happened in nearly the same order. Each day, different events were emphasized, and occasionally a new one was added. The intensity increased daily. It was as if my feelings had been locked away so securely that now they were coming out a little at a time, one piece at a time.

My body, remembering the physical violence, re-enacted it. The moment the regression began, I was off the mat and rolling, crashing about the room and beating the walls. Intense screams added to the exploding pain in my head. My throat and chest were raw and sore from the screaming and asthma. The memories were so revolting, I threw up constantly.

At "home," Babette cared for me as one would care for a frightened, terrified child, occasionally helping me to undress and hand feeding me my dinner in bed.

On one rare day of winter sunshine, the big Marilyn decided to come out. I walked to town, my head down, trying hard to think of anything but the attack. My thoughts were of my present family—of Todd, Jinger, and Missy. *But I'm too young to be married and have children. After all, I'm only eight.*

I pushed open the door to a travel agency, walked up to the counter, and bought a plane ticket for my Christmas trip home. My request came in a slow monotone with much stuttering. At the drugstore, I bought myself a jump rope. The saleswoman pushed the charge slip toward me to sign. I gripped the pen tightly and signed the big Marilyn's name in the little Marilyn's handwriting. I handed the saleswoman the slip, hoping she would accept it.

A Box of Crayons

The woman glanced at the slip and smiled at me. I turned walked stiffly out the door, and I wondered: *Will I ever return to "normal"?*

My handwriting now appears like this less than twelve hours after the journal entry on Tuesday night. This occurred about 5 a.m. on Wednesday after my "volcano" experience.

*This photo was taken during Christmas, 1980.
I am attempting to act my normal age of 44
while repressing my Sobbing Hurting Child.*

◆ 7 ◆

The Children in Conflict

Back in home in Arizona no one knew quite what to do with me at Christmas. In my stead, Missy decorated the house; my sister, Mary Sue, hostessed the big family dinner, with Jinger and Mother helping. The beloved traditions of the past faded against the stark changes my family saw in me. The perfectly decorated table and elegant dinner were there, but the outrageous stories and fond memories were replaced by awkward laughter and hushed voices that hung around the house like misplaced ornaments.

My family did not know if they should talk to me or leave me alone. I joined them for an hour or so, then retreated to a back room to sleep. My glazed eyes and stammering, deliberate speech reminded them of a mentally ill person, not the Marilyn that was a core of strength for the family. They tried to ignore the bruises on my arms from pounding the therapy floor and avoided looking at the face they had rarely seen without make-up.

I could not focus on those around me. I knew who these people were, but I could not connect them to my body, to my flesh and blood. I knew in some, now disconnected, portion of my mind that this man, Todd, was my husband. But the thought of being married seemed foreign, and Todd seemed a stranger. I also knew that I had borne these two beautiful young women, but they did not belong to me. They belonged to the big Marilyn—the one who had taken over my body for thirty-six years and used it for her own purposes.

Being with all these people consumed enormous amounts of my energy. I did not know how to take care of myself, much less how to deal with others around me. The others, so used to having me take care of them, did not know how to take care of me.

My eight-year-old was so glad to fly to California, to return to the safety of the only world I knew: to my doctor, Pete, and to my "loving care-taker," Babette. I did not like the unfamiliar outside world. It frightened me. I disliked hedges and people and anything outside the four walls of my therapy room and the four flowered walls of my bedroom at Babette's.

The therapy room was where I was reborn, where I finally made my appearance after so many years of being buried in a steel box in a snow-covered vacant lot in Kansas. I had fought underneath the surface for so many years, trying to let the big Marilyn know I existed, trying to get out of my box. I had hidden in there to be safe, so the soldiers would not find me and no one would ask me questions. I had spent many years trying to find the body that Marilyn had walked off with. Now that I had it back, I hated to let the big Marilyn use it even for Christmas.

Back "home" in Burlingame, my Original Feeling Child settled back into my body again, patting it and marveling how much it had grown without me those thirty-six years. During my sessions, my Sobbing Hurting Child emerged as long as she was able to hold my Controlling Child at bay. But my fiercely angry Controlling Child filled my nights with torment. She continued to berate me with, "I told you that to feel is to hurt! Don't listen to Pete. Listen to me!"

I was miserable, but Dr. Danylchuk was with me daily and I did listen to him. I thought of him as much more than a doctor or a teacher. He was my protector, my friend. He treated me in a gentle, loving way, just like he treated his own little girl.

During the sessions, my screams of terror reached into his father-protector and brought out his own anger, love, and concern. "I'm here," he repeated over and over. "Pete's here. They can't hurt you anymore."

Sometimes I could hear him, but I could never feel him. He could touch me, but I did not feel it. He could comfort me as he did his own small daughter, but I was locked in a steel tube that could not be penetrated. I watched him, tears rolling down my face, wishing I could feel.

By mid-January, I was able to talk in an adult voice, no longer an eight-year-old outside of my therapy sessions. Slowly, I began the long healing journey toward being an adult, an adult with the capacity to feel all feelings, appropriate and "inappropriate." I began referring to this part of myself as my Feeling Adult.

Dr. Danylchuk gradually began working with that maturing part of me during a portion of our sessions and the stronger my adult became, the deeper my child dropped. I felt myself falling like Alice in Wonderland, head over heels, heels over head, my nails broken and splintered as I clawed the slimy walls, trying to find a handhold so I would not fall any further.

I hated the things I learned as I plunged downward: the men, their cruelty examined up close; their shouts of laughter as they began the game with my terrorized child, evolving into sick suggestions, and following through with perverted actions. My little girl, afraid to die, begged my assailants to stop. As the terror progressed, I decided the pain was too terrible. I wanted to die.

My pleas to God fell on unhearing ears. In one final, excruciating moment, I saw God turn His back on me. My feelings of worth, pummeled by many large men, died with the abandonment of God. Overwhelmed, abandoned, and rejected, the little girl bowed her head in the face of death.

When death comes, it is not always the peaceful departure as described by those who have had out-of-body experiences. Sometimes it is the sheer terror of murder—a rending of the emotional, the intellectual, and the physical. And for a small child, the decision to die cannot be made easily. How does one decide to die?

When physical injury causes intolerable pain, the mind and body go into shock to protect against the fear of impending death and to conserve energy for the healing process. So, too, the emotions go into shock, splitting and creating a new personality to take over. The little girl, writhing on the ground, pushed over the edge into near insanity, found the

strength within herself to kill only her emotions—
not to die physically or intellectually, only emotionally.

To die physically would make Mommy cry. To
die intellectually was not an option for a child
raised to be smart. The only option left for little
Marilyn Reh was to die emotionally and let someone else take over the task of living and breathing.

The split came with a tearing pain, a pulling
apart that left jagged edges torn and bleeding: the
Sobbing Hurting Child and the Original Feeling
Child were buried and the Controlling Child took
over, abandoning the rest of herself in the shallow
grave.

The more of this I uncovered, the deeper into the
pit of my unconscious I fell. I would work at a consistent level for several days, pouring out my pain
until Dr. Danylchuk and I felt that I could not go
any deeper. Over his lunch hour I would rest in the
therapy room. Then suddenly I would know it was
time to drop to a new, more intense level. It was as
though God stretched out His hand and wrote on
the ceiling. It was that clear. Instinctively I would
know ahead of time which part of the attack I
would experience next.

While waiting for Dr. Danylchuk, I often played
tapes, feeling the strength and power of the words
and notes, tapes that I borrowed from other clients,
old songs, new songs, gospel songs, songs from my
childhood. Then one day, I found the song that had
so captured me as a child—Ginger's song, the one I
sang with Kay, the one that pierced my heart every
time I heard it—"You'll Never Walk Alone."

The words of the song wove in and out of my

memories—a small child walking through the dark, determined not to be afraid; the storm of the attack, the violence and helplessness; her pleas for help and her disbelief.

Like a train out of control, my anger came screaming through. "NO! The dark is awful! I DID walk alone. God wasn't there. I had hope. I trusted God. And He wasn't there."

I grabbed a soft bataca bat and pounded the wall with it. As I pounded, tears poured down my face. That song! That song that always pulled me toward a blackness I could never describe, that always brought such intense pain. Now I knew why.

I had walked home in the dark, but God was not there. I walked alone and was attacked because of it. Another puzzle piece locked into place.

Each day, at the end of the long therapy hours, Dr. Danylchuk reached his hand in the pit and pulled me up onto an invisible ledge. He tried to pull me all the way out, but it was not possible. So he lifted me as high as he could and set me on a ledge for the night. And there on that cold stone ledge, I lay, shivering in the darkness. Occasionally, a very bright light came close to my eyes and terrified me. Then it went away.

I went to sleep on the black ledge every night and woke up on the same ledge every morning. As Dr. Danylchuk arrived in the therapy room, all I had to do was lie down on the mat, breathe deeply, and I was off the ledge again, falling deeper and deeper into my memories.

Over and over, I begged him to tell me that this did not really happen, that I was crazy instead. He reassured me that my emotions confirmed what had happened. If I had made it all up, I would have no emotions connected to the thoughts. It would not make me shake, curl up in a ball, explode around the room, scream, or cry.

Each day I discovered a little bit more about the attack. More pieces to the puzzle were added. Like seeing an old movie many times, each new viewing revealed a nuance not noticed before. The movie did not change, nor did the details. It was the nuances that gave me new awareness. The puzzle became more than bits and clusters of random pieces. I now was finding the "ahh" pieces that tied them together. The complete picture had become distinct and recognizable.

Many things were confirmed in the light of reliving my eight-year-old's trauma: my unquenchable need for shoes, now owning no less than one hundred pairs, to compensate for the panic of needing to find my shoes before I could go home that tragic afternoon; the misplaced bone in the back of my skull, knocked by a severe blow.

My unconscious had used my body to try to tell my mind what had happened: asthma, which began the night of the attack, recreated the coughing and choking, the inability to breathe during oral rape; headaches, from the men holding me by the hair to complete the oral rape; and the pain in my legs. I remembered how difficult it had been sometimes to go shopping for school clothes for the girls. I had tried tennis, easy jogging, and water skiing, all to no avail. My legs were pressed into the frozen ground during the attack, growing numb and lifeless—legs that betrayed me when they could not run fast enough to get away.

I wanted more than anything to be crazy. I wanted so badly to have made it all up. But I never went to R- or X-rated movies. Violence and sexual abuse were not part of my reading or viewing material. I rarely watched television. Instead I had read book after book about the spiritual life. I wanted to have seen or heard something of such violence and perversion to have recreated it in my mind. But I had not.

It did not make sense. I didn't want it to make sense. It was far too frightening to have it all be true. How could I face my parents? How could I tell them what happened? *It will make my mommy cry and my daddy mad.* I had spent my life trying to keep pain away from my mother. My mother had watched her own mother die in a fire. *Don't make mommy more sad. Mommy has headaches. Mommy has a new baby. Mommy has lots of girls to take care of in a big house during the war. Don't give Mommy something else to trouble her.*

And God. Where the hell was God? *Why didn't He come to rescue me! Why didn't He come to help me! Was He too busy somewhere else! Or was I just so bad and so ugly that God couldn't even look at me! God didn't care. God didn't like me. He erased me.*

I found it difficult to release any anger toward my offenders. At first, I allowed myself to feel what my response would be if the victim had been Jinger or Missy; I was able to imagine fiercely defending my children. But it took several months before I was able to pick up a racquet to beat the therapy mat in defense of my own Sobbing Hurting Child.

Daily I fought with myself, trying to decide

whether or not to go on, but each day I decided I owed it to that gutsy little kid who was so determined to survive. She had fought hard to stay alive at age eight, and she did it alone. Surely I could keep her alive now. We were no longer alone.

Minimal contact with the outside world came through the mail and over the phone. I found it difficult to speak on the phone. I knew that Todd and my family needed to hear me, but I usually hung up quickly. Each day a stack of cards waited for me at the center: always, a card from my sister, Mary Sue, and regularly, a letter or card of love from my mother. The rest came from other family members, MORE THAN FRIENDS, church friends, and gallery customers. Their show of love and the assurance of their prayers for me helped me stay on my ledge and not fall into eternal oblivion.

My daily plunge deep into my unconscious left me shrouded in darkness. All sunlight disappeared from over my head. My only reality became Dr. Danylchuk, Babette, four bare walls, and a mat I never stayed on.

At the same time, my family's reality spun with as much confusion as mine. Gradually I sensed a shift in Todd's willingness to support and encourage my healing. His calls became filled with pleas for me to come home. His distress was evident as his wife went from being an extremely competent woman who could organize anything and succeed, to a woman who colored and read third-grade books; who went from being an articulate speaker and moderator for women's groups, art shows, and church functions, to a withdrawn person who spoke with the stammering voice of a frightened child with a limited vocabulary; who changed from an extremely affectionate woman, to one who shied away from his touch, who actually seemed to be afraid of his touch. I sensed he felt he was losing his partner with whom he had worked for twenty-four years, the one person who knew all the loops, tangles, and twists of our finances, his lover, his cook, and the mother of his children.

With the full responsibility of the gallery and the family on his shoulders, Todd was thrust into a world which must have been confusing and difficult. I heard that when he turned to his friends for help some encouraged him to go to California and bring his wife home. I also heard that they told him my place was at home, by his side, supporting him and his needs. Maybe the therapist did not know what he was doing. All I needed was to be in Scottsdale where those who loved me could take care of me.

Many people in our conservative world did not believe in psychologists, psychiatrists, or anyone pretending to know what secrets the mind might hold. They did not believe there could be any secrets the conscious mind did not know about. There could be no secrets, no pain, that God could not heal. While firmly believing in medical doctors for physical wounds, some of these people believed "emotional doctors" were unnecessary. Prayer and scripture covered it all.

The rest of the family was certainly affected by the stress that developed as a result of my absence. At eighteen, Missy contemplated quitting college to live with her father. During the six-week winter break, she cleaned house, cooked meals, and provided care. She felt that she was trying to hold him together, much the way a child tries to keep the ocean waves from destroying her sand castle.

Missy felt I was dying, that I would not live through the therapy. She was reminded of the months preceding my trip to Burlingame when I had walked her through the house saying, "Here's where all the photo albums are kept. Everything in the house is categorized, the silver, the art . . ."

She stuffed all her feelings of fear and apprehension and tried to take care of everything and everybody. Yet, in spite of Todd's request for her to stay with him, Missy returned to school at the end of the six weeks.

Jinger, living in Flagstaff, depended on her husband Brad for her strength. She poured her time and energy into being a wife and a mother to one-year-old B.J. It was painful for her to see her role model disintegrating; painful not to have a Mom to confide in, a Mom who could share in the excitement of a small boy's new adventures.

My parents were in constant turmoil over my situation. Guilt and sorrow consumed them. Mother wept continually. She begged to talk to me on the phone, but I was unable to talk with her. I knew I could not bear my mother's pain and mine too. Mary Sue and her family bore the weight of caring for my parents as well as dealing with their own grief and confusion.

Kay and MORE THAN FRIENDS maintained. One of our group later said, "Marilyn was like the pole, and we all revolved around her. When she left we said, 'But where do we go now? What do we do?

Who's going to take care of us?' For a time we all collapsed. It was terrible for her family and for us."

Choosing to stay in therapy, choosing to do what was best for me, was the first time in my life that I chose to do something that went against the wishes of my loved ones.

It was the most difficult, painful choice I had ever made.

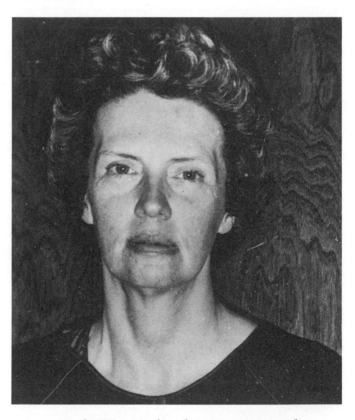

April, 1981. My face became gaunt and drawn, dotted with broken capillaries from intense screaming.

◆ 8 ◆

Slivers of Glass

Alone. Empty. Empty lots full of men and one leafless tree, all looking down on one small child. A white, naked child. Whiter against the black ground. Whiter against the black skin of the attackers.

Raw emotion choked me. Tears of fear. Tears of abandonment. "Bad, ugly, bad."

"I can't go on, Pete. I can't go on in this ugly dark room. I have to have some light, some hope, or I will die."

I did not even shudder as I thought of suicide—of almost jumping off the freeway overpass the day before, of wishing the car had not swerved to miss me that morning on the way to the center.

"Please, Pete. Please take me out in the sunshine. Take me to where I don't have to think about this attack. I'm so tired. Tired of hurting. Tired of crying. Tired of being miserable!"

He slowly shook his head. "I'm not sure it's appropriate."

"Pete, my adult's going to die in this room with my child if I don't see some sun."

He looked at my drawn face dotted with broken

capillaries from intense screaming. My clothes hung on my gaunt figure. How much weight had I lost? Twenty-five . . . thirty pounds? "You do need exercise," he said.

"I'm taking long walks now. I can even navigate a hill with ease. I rarely have a headache except during my sessions. I haven't had a single cold all winter. No asthma, no allergies, nothing. I'm getting better." I pleaded, "Please, I need something more."

"Well, let's think about it."

By the time Friday arrived, Dr. Danylchuk had agreed to a drive in the country. We traveled over winding roads and through the hills to the nearby ocean. My eyes opened wide in delight, my eight-year-old child enthralled by the beauty. "Look at the flowers!" I squealed. "And that tree is so tall. Look over there!"

Dr. Danylchuk laughed and joined in, happy to share knowledge of his beloved coast with my enthusiastic child.

Gazing at the tall trees lining the road on the trip home, I smiled. "Let's do this every Friday."

He looked at the transformed child next to him. "We'll see," he said, pleased that the outing seemed therapeutic.

The joy of the time outside quickly faded as I anticipated an upcoming visit by Todd, I did not know what to do. My adult was telling me to be a "dutiful" wife and my child was very afraid.

At Dr. Danylchuk's request, Todd came to Burlingame for three days. Todd agreed to watch one of my therapy sessions, hoping it would give him insight into the behavior of this person who was once his wife and now a stranger. When the session began, Todd watched as his wife, Marilyn Murray, slipped into the pain of Marilyn Reh, a small child immersed in a horror she could not comprehend or defend against.

Hours later, it was as though that session had not occurred. Instead, I felt pressured to respond like a wife. He was sweet and loving, and I wanted to respond in kind; however, my daily painful experiences in therapy dampened my response in our lovemaking. I could feel his anger and he wanted me to go home with him because he thought I was becoming involved with Dr. Danylchuk. That appeared to be the only reason for my reaction, and also the reason why I was continuing to stay in California. No amount of explanation of how my therapy affected me as the cause for my response to him, or assurance that Dr. Danylchuk was only my therapist, seemed to change his mind.

I returned to therapy, and at the same time I constantly questioned my decision to stay to work out the memories surrounding the attack. I felt torn between my marriage and my health. Going back to Scottsdale permanently now would mean putting on the old Marilyn, my Controlling Child, forgetting the new Original Feeling Child I was created to be.

I reflected on the previous five months and all the steps of my therapy. I remembered how my Controlling Child, the protective, defensive one who kept me alive, fought desperately to keep me from feeling, to keep me from hurting.

Through the months, I had learned that most people in regressive therapy feel the impact of their memories at approximately 30 to 50 percent of the original emotional level because their defense mechanisms are so high. It took three months of intense work for me to persuade my Controlling Child to let me go, to let me really feel. When she did, I dropped so deeply into the unconscious that I felt the attack at a full 100 percent, without the protective benefit of shock.

At first, I could feel the attack only in a split way; I experienced either the physical or the emotional aspects of the attack, keeping them separate as one separates the yolk of an egg from the white.

Originally the attack had emerged with an enormous amount of physical movement. These body memories accompanied the violent flashbacks. I felt the attack physically as my child had experienced it, all the kicking and the tossing, the confusion and the hysterical fear. While they were intense feelings, they were "safer" feelings.

Gradually my emotions intensified to include all the feelings of the attack. Instead of being cast violently about the room, I spent hours huddled in a corner, screaming and sobbing. I felt terror, loneliness, ugliness, guilt, pain, abandonment, and rejection by God. I felt totally powerless, overwhelmed, and outnumbered.

I had dreaded the day I had to experience the physical and the emotional together. With the release of my Controlling Child, my physical and emotional pain joined in a collision so violent that I thought I had finally reached the bottom of the pit. I was mistaken. I had just begun my descent.

It took months to drop to the point where I could allow myself to feel the attack and face it with all the cognition of an adult: accept that it had happened to me—to this face, to this mouth, to this Marilyn Murray—not just to some little girl I did not know, to a nameless body lying on the dirty ground in Kansas thirty-six years ago.

The blessed ignorance of the eight-year-old had protected me from all the attack meant. My little girl did not know what oral rape was. She did not understand they had attempted anal rape. But the adult Marilyn was faced with the full truth. I forced myself to feel the horror, the repulsion, and the disgust of what the men's vile acts meant to my body. The truth caused me to vomit over and over and over again.

I responded physically and emotionally as though I was an adult who was being gang raped for several hours every day. The experience of that rape no longer affected me only in my sessions. The effects were the same as if it had actually happened that day. Physically, I looked like a woman who had been totally ravaged. Emotionally, I could no longer separate the reality of the therapy room from the reality of the everyday world. My Sobbing Hurting Child merged completely with my adult.

Part of experiencing the whole of the attack included reliving the split. Intellectually, I knew this defense mechanism saved my life. Emotionally, the severe pain of splitting tore at me and doubled my body over in agonizing torture. How could anyone, especially an eight-year-old, make such a vital decision, choosing between life and death? To choose to kill a portion of your treasured self for survival— would it be better to die a whole person or to live as a fragmented one? How can decisions like that be made?

I poured out the agony in my journal:

> 'Don't make me do this . . . I don't want to kill myself!'

> The glow of the street light prowls through the barren trees. It casts a dark shadow upon the kneeling figure rocking back and forth in the snow. A wail pierces the air and hangs suspended in time as she mourns the dead child clutched in her arms.

Dr. Danylchuk listened and understood. He cared, he supported, and he reinforced my self-esteem. I liked it all, except for his words about God. He asked if I might be angry at God. But anger had never been acceptable to me, and anger toward God was unthinkable. Then he would say, "In order to have a genuine relationship with anyone, including God, it needs to be an honest one. We can't repair a relationship until we acknowledge that it's broken."

But the bottom of the pit had not yet been reached. When I hit bottom, it came as a thirteen-story fall, slamming me against the frozen, black, dirty ground. As a child, I had counted on one, all-powerful being to rescue me, at least to be there with me: the God of all children, the God who puts children on his lap to cuddle and protect them. When all hope had gone, I still held hope in that good, great, and powerful God.

As the attack dragged on and on it became painfully clear that God had abandoned me. I was so ugly, so worthless, I felt that God had simply pretended I did not exist.

The volcano blew again. During the many years of sitting in church, years of teaching my children and friends that God loved them and had grace in abundance for them, the volcano had boiled. It churned very deep below the surface, red, massive, seething—angry at being contained, angry that flowers were planted and homes built over it, pretending it did not exist.

Pure, raw hatred exploded and poured over the sides of the carefully manicured mountain, destroying everything in its path. "God, I HATE YOU!"

A loving God who protects children from harm?
"NO!"
A caring God who loves you no matter what?
"NO! HE ERASED ME."
A God who is soft and loving?
"NO!
"God, YOU let them do that to me! I HATE YOU!
"Are you blind? Can't you see? How could you let this happen to such a little child?!"

The anger spilled forth and was spent. I lay in a mound, huddled on the floor, breathing hard.

As I regained my strength and sat up, Dr. Danylchuk began to answer my questions. "I think God cried for you during your attack. I know He didn't want it to happen any more than you did. It's hard for anyone to understand how God allows evil and tragedy in the world. A partial understanding is that He has given human beings free choice. He does not control their actions. On the other hand, God can make His healing love available to us directly, or more often through people."

I walked to Babette's, my mind reeling with those words. All the "ifs" poured into me. If I had not met Kay, there would have been no prayers for her. If Kay had not found peace with God, she would never have read Cecil Osborne's book. If she had never read Dr. Osborne's book, there might have been MORE THAN FRIENDS, but they would not have known Dr. Osborne and the center. If Kay and I had not fought, Kay would never have gone to Burlingame. If Kay had never gone, I would never have been encouraged, no, forced to go for help.

The hedges loomed tall and dark alongside me as I walked. The inner child recoiled, waiting for the arms like steel bands to circle my chest again. I swallowed hard, held my chin up, and walked on by.

God had orchestrated my healing. He put me here with the right therapist. Dr. Danylchuk's experience in regressive therapy and doctorate in pastoral psychotherapy combined two worlds successfully. I needed someone who understood my spirituality as well as my damaged emotions.

I looked into the trees bursting with spring growth. *The trees had no leaves. The black and dirty ground.* I looked around me at the new life—flowers, and lush grass carpeting front yards. I looked from the winter of my sorrow into the spring of new life. *Maybe God does care about a naked, terrorized, hysterical, battered child.*

I felt like a crystal vase that had been shattered and was now being put back together by a caring, patient individual, someone who would take time to gather all the tiny pieces and figure out how they fit together. It would take many, many long hours to put that vase together again. But with patience, love, and concern, it was being accomplished.

When a crystal vase shatters, slivers of glass can imbed themselves in the skin, cutting and stinging. With those slivers, the vase lets others know a portion of the pain it endured. The vase, humbled and embarrassed by its shattering, does not want anyone to know its fragility. After being pieced together, the vase feels weak and ugly.

My vase trembled in its fragility. There were still some missing fragments. The glue was not yet dry.

It was time to prepare to go home. It was time to go back into the real world as a new person, in reality the person I was created to be. My therapy had revealed my fears of abandonment, my fears of being lost without the craftsman who put me back together: Dr. Danylchuk, the only one who knew the real vase. Everyone in Arizona knew a clay pot that had hidden the broken pieces of Marilyn Reh for thirty-six years. They did not know the crystal vase. *What if they don't like who I am? Will they accept the fragility?*

Dr. Danylchuk and I worked hard, rehearsing the future and its possibilities. We discussed Todd's recent visit to Burlingame and his response. Pete had recommended marriage counseling as an essential part of my eventual return home. While in Burlingame Todd had agreed, but he changed his mind after returning to Arizona. During our phone calls, I felt that he wanted me to return to Arizona as if nothing had happened in my therapy, as if I could just be the wife I had been before my work with Dr. Danylchuk.

I cradled the phone on my shoulder, my hands

shaking as I lived my new role. "Todd, I need you to support me in this. I need you to go to a counselor with me. Our marriage depends on it."

This was difficult to understand. We had had many wonderful years together without counseling. Why should we need it now? I think he saw problems in our marriage, but they were nothing that proper spirituality, on my part, could not fix.

Dr. Danylchuk also arranged for me to begin a slow re-entry with several brief visits to Arizona as I neared the end of the intensive phase of my therapy. My re-entry began on Easter, 1981, a very fitting time for me—Resurrection Sunday. It was also Todd's and my twenty-fifth wedding anniversary.

I delighted in seeing my family. I looked at little B.J. and pledged I would do everything in my power to allow him to grow up free, free to feel. But this brief visit gave me only glimpses of what it would be like for me and for those I loved upon my permanent return.

During my last month in Burlingame I wrote to Todd. When he had read my letter, I was sure he would not be pleased. Perhaps he might hope I would come to my senses and return sooner than planned. Instead, I let my true feelings show, something I had seldom done in our marriage. At last I was being appropriately assertive. I told him about my hurt over his reaction toward my therapy. It felt as if I had slapped him in the face. I could sense his anger and frustration.

The pain flowed through me as a rushing river. When it slowed to a trickle, I wrote another letter. I addressed his concerns and then set out the new framework within which I felt comfortable to function. I refused to take inappropriate responsibility for his feelings, but promised to be a separate individual in a healthy, growing marriage.

Part Three

Reclaiming the Original Feeling Child

♦ 9 ♦

The Return

October, 1988. I sat mesmerized in front of my VCR watching *Empire in the Sun*. It is the story of a young boy raised in a wealthy British family in China at the start of World War II. He is a bright eyed, slightly spoiled, naive child. As he is chauffered through the teeming streets of Shanghai, he watchs beggars, homeless children, and Japanese soldiers whirl by. He remains isolated and protected by the big car in which he rides.

When the war breaks out, his simple world is torn apart, and he is separated from his parents. He spends most of the war in a Japanese concentration camp, with brutality, hunger, and death as part of his daily experiences. His life becomes a matter of surviving.

At the end of the movie, the boy is finally reunited with his parents. Looking haggard and pale, he holds back at first, still locked in the painful prison of his last few years. Then he cautiously reaches up and touches his mother's face and hair. At last he allows her to hug him, and the scene closes with him laying his head on her shoulder and very slowly closing his eyes—safe at last.

I cried throughout much of the movie, but the last scene hit me so hard that I sobbed aloud. It was the first thing I had seen that showed how I felt when I returned home to Arizona after my therapy. I had been a prisoner of war, and neither I nor my family and friends realized it.

I backed up the videotape and watched the last scene again. I imagined what it would be like to try to place that war-ravaged boy in an ordinary classroom filled with average kids his age. His classmates' realm of experience—the boundaries they lived within—would be radically different from his. His experience would be light years away from those of "average kids." He had been catapulted beyond his frontier, into a totally foreign territory, and he had learned to survive in that terrifying place. Somehow playing ball or flying toy airplanes would never fit again.

As I played the final scene over and over, I was awash with the pain of the memories of my own homecoming, yet amazed and intrigued by the revelation before me. At last I had a clear insight into what had happened to me and my family when I returned from Burlingame.

The boy in the movie felt "safe at last," but I had not come home to a safe, protected place. I came home to an angry, confused husband and a community where I no longer fit. My family and friends loved me, but they did not understand me.

It was not their fault. I could not blame them, any more than I could blame a Kansas farm family unable to understand their son upon his return from a POW camp in Luzon or Mindanao after World War II.

The Return

The night my "volcano" blew in December 1980, I was liberated from my steel box, my solitary confinement. While I was no longer confined in that desolate place within my mind, neither was I free. I was still in a prison. It took another seven months in intensive therapy to work myself out of that prison, to get to a place where I could finally feel strong enough to walk out past the gates into freedom.

I returned home to Scottsdale on June 21, 1981, knowing what it was like to be free. Not only was I now out of my prison, my former boundaries, like the boy's, had also been blown into oblivion. For months I had been walking a new frontier, a frontier so foreign, so strange, that it was beyond the comprehension of anyone I knew besides my friends in Burlingame.

Remembering and re-experiencing gang rape hour after hour, listening to a child's terrorized screams, realizing with horror that those screams belong to you: these are things the "average" person does not want to hear about. These are things no one wants to admit ever happen, especially not to someone they know and love.

No one wanted to believe that Dachau existed either. Even when actual photographs were given to our government, the officials could not accept that anyone could or would do such things to other human beings.

In 1981, the majority of this country did not want to believe sexual abuse actually happened and that it could be as horrendous and as frequent as the reports that were gradually surfacing. Rather than believe, it was easier to speculate, to doubt, to question.

When I returned to Scottsdale, nearly everyone saw the "new Marilyn" as a different person from the one who had departed three seasons prior. Rumors of "a nervous breakdown," "psychotic break," "an affair," "self-centered," "selfish," "unspiritual," and so on followed me wherever I went and would not let me be.

It was not acceptable for me to be free in Arizona at that time. Freedom for me meant having a healthy personal boundary surrounding me, instead of being part of the collective boundary of our culture—an all encompassing boundary in which each individual's boundary was permeable for others to invade at will.

♦ ♦ ♦

June, 1981. Strained smiles were painted on the faces of my family as they greeted me at the airport. As I received their loving hugs, I had no way of knowing the conflict my presence would cause in the ensuing months, no way to know they would have so much difficulty accepting everything the new Marilyn stood for and desired. It seemed so simple to my newly emerged Original Feeling Child: Just let me be free to be me.

I left Burlingame knowing that one hour of an attack had changed my whole life. Before the attack, I already had several patterns in my life—patterns of not wanting to make my mother cry and of not knowing how to deal with anger—and the attack reinforced those patterns. There were also many new patterns because of the attack: always trying to be perfect, for to make a mistake—like reading on the bus—meant total annihilation; a strong need to be in control to counter my feelings of being overpowered and helpless; being afraid to talk back because it might cause me to be severely injured; always looking for a protector, a female "stronger than me but not a mommy"; avoiding conflict at all costs; and allowing my body to express my emotions through physical pain. Most of all, I was trying to prove to God, myself, and the world that I was not bad. *But I must have been bad, or God wouldn't have let this happen.*

Easing back into the old relationships felt uncomfortable and homey at the same time. I felt like a tightrope walker, trying to keep my balance while others shook the rope. At home it felt as if everyone followed me around, afraid to let me out of their sight. Perhaps they had missed me. Perhaps curiosity kept them following me.

My mother, filled with love for a daughter and consumed by guilt, wanted desperately to talk to me about the past. Day after day, her face was troubled with pain. I felt responsible for her tears and sleepless nights, yet I could not do what she asked.

"Mom, I can't talk to you."

Her eyes welled up with tears. She rested her soft, gentle hand on my arm. "Please, Honey. Please talk to me."

"I can't, Momma. Every time I try, you cry. And I can't handle your tears. It's too painful for me. I had to seek professional help for my pain, Momma. I can't carry yours and mine too."

Mary Sue called and encouraged me to talk to my mother.

Jinger called and encouraged me to talk to my mother.

Missy called and encouraged me to talk to my mother.

I stayed in my house, not wanting to risk going outside. If I did, I might run into my mother and father. Then I would have to face the effect my absence had on them. I loved them so much but hated to see the hurt I had caused them.

I looked forward to church on Sunday where I could see all those who so faithfully supported me in prayer. Walking close behind Todd, I could hide from the noise and confusion facing me.

In church, I hoped to repair my damaged relationship with God. I still loved Him, but I had experienced so much rage and confusion, wondering how He could love me and still allow the horrendous attack to take place. I knew I had to forgive God for His choices concerning me. I had to forgive God for abandoning me as a little girl.

I also felt incredible gratitude that my therapy with Dr. Danylchuk had allowed God's healing love to begin its work in that little girl's heart. I was grateful that God had provided a therapy center—a sanctuary far from home, where I would not have to go home daily to a family and adult responsibilities after reliving my nightmare as an eight-year-old.

As I looked at the people in the church aisles, talking and laughing, I felt so at home and so out of place at the same time. I wondered what had been said about me and how I should respond. I wanted to go home and cry. I wanted to stay and greet those who had loved me for so many years and had spent seven months praying for me.

I was confused. Everything seemed to be in conflict. Daily, I scolded myself for feeling I had a right to survive. I berated myself for not sacrificing my own well-being and welfare for my husband.

I am sure it was confusing for Todd, he probably did not know whether to be happy or angry. One moment I would hear how pleased he was at the new health I had, and the next, I would hear his anger and frustration that the "old Marilyn" had been taken from him. I lived in fear of stirring up more anger and frustration. The attack had taught me: *If I protect myself, I'll get hurt more.*

I mentally shook myself and tried to remaster the old tapes that spun around in my head. At the same time, I clung to my new vision of marriage, a life of mutual respect, not a one-up, one-down relationship.

Life had continued in Arizona for seven months without my presence, but those in my life had been so used to my being in charge that many things had been left undone. In September, I felt I was finally ready to return to my duties as bookkeeper for our business. I brought the ledgers and files home from the gallery in a box four feet long, two feet wide and a foot high. *It looks just like a coffin,* I thought. *My coffin.*

Dr. Danylchuk had suggested that I avoid as much stress as possible for a year. This sadly became a bad joke. The fragile vase, the tiny pieces barely in place with the glue not quite dry, was placed in the middle of a danger zone—in the middle of a toyless room full of toddlers, in the middle of a mighty hurricane.

When I was alone, I cried—not the tears of one moved by an emotional story, not the tears of one who has met the stinging remarks of a friend, but tears of agony, tears locked up for thirty-six years, tears for so many years of hollowness.

Unfortunately I gave into pressure and the lack of support. Gradually I fell back into the old patterns of caring for Todd's needs first, of trying to keep him happy, and of denying my own needs and how I felt.

The pain that had ceased while I was in Burlingame now came rushing back: headaches, legaches, stomach cramps, all of it flooding in and overwhelming me. In prior years, the pain had been a constant, unwelcome companion. It was a companion I could not avoid, and so I accepted it. But now, after months of being free from the excruciating pain, I knew how much better life was without it. I was angry that the old foe had returned to haunt me, but I did not know what to do to avoid it. I was determined never to take another pain pill.

My headaches eased and I was encouraged when Todd consented to enter marriage counseling with Dr. Terry Kriesel, a therapist that Dr. Danylchuk recommended. While we were there to confront the problems that had arisen from my sexual abuse issues and the resulting therapy, I also felt that we had twenty-five years of pent up frustration from not knowing how to communicate appropriately. In both our personal life and our business life we seldom resolved negative issues in a healthy way.

In addition to our marriage counseling I was

scheduled to go back to Burlingame for follow-up personal therapy. "It's like having radiation treatment after radical cancer surgery," explained Dr. Danylchuk to Todd and me.

It was clear to me that Todd did not want me to leave. For him, our relationship was the number-one priority.

I felt myself crumble. "But Todd, if I don't take care of myself, I won't live long enough to be here to work on the marriage." I was not able to help him understand that to "sacrifice myself for our marriage" would destroy the relationship we were trying to rescue.

Despite Todd's protests, I returned to Burlingame. I was determined to hold on to both my health and my relationship with Todd. I sat in a chair in Dr. Danylchuk's office and said, "Whatever I have to mold myself into, I will do so to save my marriage."

With concern in his eyes, Dr. Danylchuk asked, "Since your return home, what happened to your Original Feeling Child you worked so hard to allow to come out?"

"She's dying," I replied.

Dr. Danylchuk leaned forward as he said, "How about you and Todd, are you allowing him to take care of himself?"

"It's hard for me to let him do that. I've taken care of him all these years. But I'm beginning to understand that as long as I 'kiss it and make it well' for him, I will get in the way of him taking responsibility for his own actions."

The week passed, free from pain but full of hard

work. My return home, back into the maelstrom, brought the pain back almost instantly.

I can't bear the pain alone.

I can feel Todd's resentment toward my therapy, but I'm still not finished.

Sometimes the hostility I feel from him scares me and makes me want to run away, the way I wanted to run from the attackers.

I can't stay in Burlingame. I can't stay home. It's much easier to die.

Yet, I began to realize that the will to live, to survive, was not something I simply one day chose to do. Instead, survival was choosing to live for one day. Then for days and weeks following, I chose to die. Then I would choose again, for one short day, to live. Gradually, the days I wanted to live outnumbered the days I wanted to die. My desire to survive grew stronger than the temptation to die. I no longer felt erased by God. I took little steps forward—never giant ones, always teeny, tiny steps.

Several bright spots encouraged me to go on. My relationship with Kay had changed. No longer did I see Kay as my protector. Kay could now be a friend. Even though Kay felt some resentment toward my absence and all the responsibility left to her to run MORE THAN FRIENDS, a healthy relationship between us was emerging.

At the annual Ice Cream Social of MORE THAN FRIENDS I struggled with knowing how to act. The adult Marilyn felt such joy at seeing all my old friends. I gladly received their hugs and heard of their prayers for me during my absence. The child Marilyn hung back behind Kay, not certain of how to deal with a roomful of people. The adult Marilyn wondered at what my friends must think. The old Marilyn would have waltzed into the room, initiated hugs and conversation, served and waited on others. The new Marilyn stood to one side, hesitant, quiet, and willing to be served.

In the ensuing months, the conflicts with MORE THAN FRIENDS surprised me. Many women were still waiting for new groups to start. The established groups were anxious for new material. They were eager for me to be back at the helm. They needed and expected me to resume my old roles, but I was learning to take care of myself. Taking care of myself meant I needed an extended rest from responsibilities. The women tried to understand, but it was difficult all the way around.

The seven months in Burlingame had allowed my child to let loose and play. My Friday therapy sessions in the sun taught me to open my eyes and see life around me. My playful child encouraged me to take a trip to Lake Powell with my family. The woman who never learned to water ski because of the weakness in her legs, jet skied over a hundred miles in three days. I slept in the bow of a boat and climbed a mountain "just because it was there." From the top, I felt exhilarated. The mountain signified more than just being able to use my legs beyond walking; it signified all the hard work and valleys and pits I had worked through to come out on top.

Spiritually, my life changed. Before therapy, I had pleaded daily with God to show me His will for my life. I lived in constant panic, wondering if I was in or out of God's will. I taught salvation by grace but lived salvation by works. Now I had learned about unconditional love. I had an entirely new peace of mind and heart.

For the first time in my life, I understood what grace was really all about. I smiled more in the presence of God. I smiled, happier because I chose to become more healthy in body, mind, and soul, growing toward the person I was created to be. My Original Feeling Child was continuing on a path toward being a fully Feeling Adult.

Those around me perceived the change as slipping backward, as choosing a more "humanistic" approach to life. They noticed I did not spend as much time in concentrated prayer or Bible reading.

Understanding the concern of those who loved me, I wrote in my journal:

> I'm beginning to realize how much Todd and I are products of our generation (the 50's), our heritage (Midwest, Bible Belt, fundamentalist), and our culture (macho man with submissive wife); and how difficult it is to sort out the facets that are destructive and still keep the tenets we cherish and love, especially when we cannot agree upon which are which.

My relationship with Todd continued to flip-flop. One minute it was sweet and loving and the next minute, there was anger at all that had happened to me and how that affected our life together. I could tell that he just wanted his old wife back, without the headaches.

Well-meaning friends met with Todd, telling him that Satan had caused my childhood attack in order to destroy MORE THAN FRIENDS by having me leave to go into therapy. They said my therapy was not under God's guidance because I leaned on man, not God. They told Todd that he and I were under Satanic attack and needed fifty or sixty people to pray for us.

When Todd relayed this to me, he did so apologetically. I screamed, "When I die, I stand before God alone, not with a husband, with a pastor, a therapist, or anyone else. I alone am accountable to God for me. How dare they attempt to judge what is satanic and what is ordained by God! I agree the men in my attack went against God's will, but I believe that God, not Satan, orchestrated my healing. I so appreciated everyone's prayers for me while I was gone. But now their concern is intrusive!"

October 1981, Florence Littauer, a close friend and one of the persons who supported me in prayer during the long months of therapy, encouraged me to attend her Christian Leaders and Speakers Seminar (CLASS). The seminar taught people how to speak to groups and to use their talents and life experiences to help others. I hesitated. I was still not comfortable in public. It terrified me to think of standing in front of a group of strangers telling them what had happened to me, yet something told me God wanted me to do this. Helping someone else might make some sense out of the horror and make my pain and confusion worthwhile.

My sister, Mary Sue, and a few others from MORE THAN FRIENDS planned to attend. I put on my best dress and make-up. With tears streaking down my face, I told my story. Trembling, clutching the podium to hold myself together, I made it through.

The women responded with hurts of their own.

It baffled me to think these women could actually get something positive and helpful from my story.

Possibilites for the future filtered into my mind, and they frightened me. I felt very small. *Sometimes I wish I could just run away and be a nondescript person that no one paid any attention to.*

Throughout the coming months I often considered disappearing into the woodwork. But little things kept pulling me back—Linda in particular. As a member of the same church and also of MORE THAN FRIENDS, Linda had watched my life with intense interest. She, too, had excruciating headaches. She had waited impatiently for me to return from therapy to see if it had helped. Her observations said yes, I was a different person. The change in me gave her hope that maybe therapy was the answer for her, too.

She called and asked to talk with me. I hesitated. Although regressive therapy had been my saving grace, I knew it was not necessarily the kind of therapy everyone could benefit from. I talked with Linda and simply shared what happened with me. She requested Dr. Danylchuk's phone number and address. She looked me directly in the eyes and said, "I can't thank you enough. I think you may have saved my life!"

I went to my room that evening and prayed. "Lord, what are you doing? This isn't the direction I had intended my life to go. What are you planning for me?"

I was no longer able to do all I had done before. I was no longer driven to be perfect or to take care of the whole world. No longer could I be available for everyone. I was struggling to regain my health—

physically, emotionally, and spiritually. I was certain that God had directed my healing thus far, but I also knew I still had difficulty with the issue of trust. From deep inside me, sometimes a little voice would say, *God walked away from me that snowy afternoon; He didn't take care of me.*

♦ 10 ♦

Eager Faces and Earthquakes

In the following months, my Original Feeling
Child often wanted to skip happily down the path,
but my Sobbing Hurting Child hung back lament-
ing, "Dr. Danylchuk says we're supposed to take it
easy for a long time. I still hurt." My Controlling
Child continued to fuss at the other two. She constantly revived my old tapes: "You're being too
selfish. You should be busy taking care of others;
that way you won't have time to feel." My slowly
maturing Feeling Adult kept busy juggling the
other three. Breaking new ground was not going to
be easy.

All the "children" faced a Todd who seemed
confused about how to respond. As I worked on my
emotional growth, I begged Todd to come along
too, to see the original Marilyn, to join her in her
zest for life. But he refused.

Our marriage became a battle of wills. Todd
wanted to preserve my old role of being there for
him. I wanted what I considered to be a true marriage: a partnership that allowed both people to
become who God meant them to be, not one "becoming" and the other dying. I wanted a mutually

nurturing environment. I asked Todd to note the things he did that increased my stress and caused me physical pain. I pleaded with him to pay attention to his own physical pain, which was increasing daily and to take care of himself.

I knew that I had to choose life for myself over sacrifice for Todd. I needed to make sense out of the incredible awfulness of the attack and bring some good out of evil. I decided the goals I set for myself would benefit Todd and me, not just him.

I understood his perspective that my goals seem to mean I would have a life separate from his. But I could not always fit into his plans as I thought he wanted for me to do. Yet I am sure he believed he could have a life separate from me; that is a man's right, not a woman's.

Intertwined with the straining and groaning marriage were other problems. Todd wanted me back working with him in the gallery, yet we disagreed on how it should be run.

An opportunity arose in December for me to return to my former position as a respected art dealer. One of my oldest and best clients, Bob Parker from Oklahoma, was interested in several of our paintings, and I agreed to take them to him.

I looked forward to the drive alone, with time to sort through my thoughts. The pavement unrolled, a ribbon of asphalt beneath the spinning tires. I had made this drive to Parker Drilling in Tulsa many times in the past. Never before had the signs bothered me so.

WICHITA.

I gripped the wheel, trying to focus on the precious cargo of paintings in the back. Then, another sign.

WICHITA.

Why Lord! Why this week!

The rain clouds gathered, moving, churning, storming, matching my inner whirl.

It's cold and dirty and the trees have no leaves.

The road blurred through the icy rain and through the tears pouring from my eyes. I never thought this trip would be so difficult.

At noon, I walked into the restaurant to meet Bob and Cissy Parker. I was genuinely happy to see them again. They greeted me with warm hugs. Bob asked immediately, "So, Marilyn, why haven't we seen you in a while?"

"I've been in a therapy center in California for seven months."

Cissy placed her hand on my arm. "I'm sorry, we didn't know."

I toyed with my salad a moment, wondering if I should tell them what had happened. I looked into their friendly, loving faces and laid my fork down. "While there, I uncovered a sexual attack at age eight."

I fielded questions and answered them openly and honestly as I saw their eagerness and concern.

Bob spoke softly. "That explains a lot. I've sent several people to your gallery, telling them to ask for you. They came back and said you weren't there. No one at the gallery offered any information about where you were."

He paused as he looked me full in the face. "I'm so sorry to hear what happened to you. But I am delighted to see you looking so well!" Cissy agreed.

Bob continued, "I have some women in my office who are having difficult times right now. Divorces, kids on drugs, etc. Would you be willing to talk to them at lunch tomorrow?"

"How many?"

"Five or six."

I hesitated. A quick prayer flashed through my mind. "Well," I began slowly, "I have told only one other group about what happened to me. But I really want to help others if I can."

His instant smile encouraged me.

I continued, "I need to tell you something more. Tomorrow is going to be an exceptionally rough day for me. It will be a year to the day since I first experienced the memory of my attack. For some reason God has me here in Tulsa, a place that looks and feels just like Wichita."

The following morning, I wondered why I had ever agreed to talk to the group of women. *Only five or six*, I reassured myself. *I can handle five or six.*

I entered the meeting room. To my astonishment, more than one hundred women were waiting for their guest speaker to arrive. Bob did not give me a chance to panic. He introduced me and then stepped back from the podium.

I looked into the crowd of eager faces. I breathed a prayer of thanksgiving for the training I had received from Florence Littauer and the seminar in October. Then the first words spilled out of my mouth, "No, no, not me. I had a perfect childhood."

From the first words to the last, the audience was fully attentive. When I finished, the women swarmed around me, wanting private appointments with me. Questions pounded me, fast and furious, begging to be answered. "How do you forgive God?" "How do you deal with anger appropriately?" "How can you forgive your attackers?" "How can you be 'you' when others force you into their mold?"

Bob, surprised by the response, opened an office in the executive suite for me to meet with the hurting women. I changed my plans to leave that afternoon and listened to the women's questions and concerns. They followed me everywhere: into the bathrooms, the elevators, the lunchroom.

The men at Parker Drilling requested a chance to hear me also, and so I spoke again. Their interest surprised me. They, too, wanted to talk. They wanted to find help for the deep hurts in their lives.

A week after I arrived in Tulsa, I drove home. It did not matter that the paintings had not sold. Instead, I thought of the incredible number of hurting people and their open and warm response to the story of my attack and therapy. Somehow this trip, too, was a part of God's plan for my healing.

My head spun. Just one year ago I relived the terror of my eight-year-old and was forced to restructure every fiber of my life. My world as I knew it blew apart. Now this. *I don't understand!* I cried, *Lord, what in the world are you getting me into! It feels like an uncharted wilderness and this new frontier has no road map.*

Snow spattered my windshield and a relentless wind shook my car. I looked at the trees with no leaves. It did not matter; in a few months they would bud again. I pondered the reason for the cycle of death and rebirth, the cycle of destruction and new growth. *Today, I'm not only alive, but I'm being used to help others. I do have a purpose, a reason to live.*

Several days after my return home Todd and I had a marriage counseling session with Dr. Kriesel. After five months of discussion about our marital problems we reached a stalemate and our counseling was discontinued.

I began 1982 with a follow-up trip to Burlingame. It had become a haven outside the insanity of my world. In Burlingame, I could be myself. There my pain level retreated to zero, and I could concentrate on my therapy sessions. My present-day problems created feelings which immediately drug me back into the pain of my past, feelings of abandonment, frustration, fear, anger, and being totally overwhelmed.

During this particular trip to Burlingame, I allowed myself to re-experience the attack for the first time during a group session. The other group members sat on their floor pillows, absorbed in the intensity of my attack. They voiced their concerns, stating how minor their problems seemed compared to what I had lived through.

My Sobbing Hurting Child looked around the room, distraught by the thought that these hurting people might discount their own pain. "Please don't compare my pain to yours and feel yours is insignificant. Each of us has been deeply damaged and severely scarred. The traumas causing the wound may vary, but every person's pain is maximum to them."

That evening, as I walked back to Babette's, I realized that, although the attack was a terrible experience in my life and reliving it was one of the most painful things that had ever happened to me, I had found reasons to live and survive. I walked through the darkness, likening it to walking through my present pain with Todd. I tipped my head back to look at the faint stars. *It's so dark in my life right now. Will the morning ever come!*

Home had not changed when I returned from Burlingame. I knew it would not, but I secretly hoped it had.

As my "children" trekked across my frontier in Arizona, an earthquake had begun to rumble. Chasms opened beneath me. It felt as though my children were again being buried.

This time it was by mountains of bookkeeping. Savage headaches tore at my skull. Chest pain crushed me. Once again I crumpled on the closet floor. I pressed my fist into my chest, trying to ease the pain enough to breathe. My Sobbing Hurting Child beat the floor and cried, "God, why are you allowing this to happen to me again? It's not fair!"

Somehow I knew fair had nothing to do with it. God never promised life would be fair. He never promised a life without pain. But that did not stop me from asking, asking, asking to be released from the pain.

The doctors, again, had no evidence as to the cause of my pain. All test results were negative. The cardiologist peered over his bifocals and my chart. "Mrs. Murray, what are your stresses presently?"

I began to list them, ticking off on my fingers each major stressor.

The doctor shook his head. "Unless you drastically modify your situation, you will continue to experience severe pain and possibly future problems."

I left his office, glad for the negative test results, yet concerned about the stresses over which I had no control.

While my body had reverted to its physical state prior to therapy, my soul had begun to grow and thrive. My "children" were determined not to stay buried in the rubble of the chaos around me. My Feeling Adult reached in and started to pull them out. It was time to make some healthy decisions.

I returned to Dr. Kriesel. I had not seen him since Todd and I had discontinued our therapy several months previously. After the seven months in Burlingame, I knew my physical pain was closely connected to my emotional pain. I hoped that a session with Dr. Kriesel would help me sort out what emotional problems were affecting my physical well-being.

Dr. Kriesel considered the pain etched into my face. He leaned forward in his chair as he spoke, "Marilyn, what is your life worth to you? The sign on my door says I am a marriage counselor. I am in the business of saving marriages. But my first priority is *saving lives.* You and Todd absolutely have to get into counseling again if you are going to survive. If you and Todd do not feel comfortable seeing me that's okay but find somebody right away."

On my way home, I stopped to see an old friend of Todd's and mine. He welcomed me into his office. I asked if he would talk to Todd for me.

I said, "Maybe you can convince Todd that without some kind of help from a counselor, I will have to leave in order to stay alive."

Our friend responded, "I will talk to him. I even have a friend I can recommend. I have worked with him. He is a great marriage counselor."

Within a few days, Todd approached me with the idea of beginning counseling with a therapist he was willing to see named Dr. Ralph Earle.

Maybe, just maybe, I would not be traveling on my new frontier all alone. The news gave my hopes a new birth. It did not make the other stressors go away, but for a moment it made them a little easier to cope with. Hope and support.

The rumbling of the earthquake quieted for a time.

◆ 11 ◆

Swamps and Bikinis

I could not sit still. "What am I going to do, Pete? I don't know who to refer these hurting people to besides you." I moved restlessly about the room. "And what was this thing that happened to me? The 'split'? I want to know and understand it all."

Dr. Danylchuk looked at me with a knowing smile and said, "Have you thought about going back to school?"

"What?"

"Go back to school. You might consider a degree in psychology."

Thoughts of returning to school brought visions of battling crowds of teenagers in parking lots and classrooms, standing in long lines to register for classes, spending years attending classes. I shook my head. "It's not for me."

Dr. Danylchuk smiled. "If you put it that way, no it's not. But there are legitimate, accredited colleges that will give you credit for prior learning. Check around your area and see what you can find."

I discovered Ottawa University in Phoenix. Ironically, their home campus was in Kansas.

I attended the first interview prepared to be disappointed, but the meeting far exceeded my expectations. They treated me as an adult, understood my specific needs, and knew how to help me. My first assignment was to attend an introductory class one night a week for eight weeks.

The first night I looked around the room, acutely aware this was the first time I would be interacting with strangers on a consistent basis since my return from therapy. Knowing my fragility, I questioned my ability to maintain my balance between the present and the past.

Swallowing hard, I sat in the only seat available, next to a black gentleman in his midfifties. I discovered that he had been stationed in the Midwest during World War II for army training. Thoughts of the attack flashed through my mind, but I quieted them and focused on getting to know this man. I found him to be kind and gentle. It pleased me that my healing had reached the point where I was capable of being friends with him.

The following day, Todd and I had a very difficult discussion. I was enthusiastic in recounting my new experiences at school. For me it was the fulfillment of a lifelong goal. Todd did not see my return to school in the same way. However I was encouraged again by our new beginning with Dr. Ralph Earle who I was also seeing for personal therapy as well as couple counseling.

I often felt like I was trudging through a murky swamp filled with quicksand, falling in, struggling to reach for help. Dr. Earle, Dr. Danylchuk, Jinger, Missy, Mary Sue, Cynthia Morse, a new friend who was a therapist in Dr. Earle's office, my MORE THAN

FRIENDS group—I needed to find people willing and strong enough to help me up and out.

My Sobbing Hurting Child never seemed to go away. She was always there, crying in the background, letting me know she still felt swamped— swamped by her frustration over Todd, by her increasing physical pain, by problems at the gallery, by her concern over her parents, by the rumors she heard about herself. The rumors grew more unpleasant by the day.

Most people did not understand the pain. They were not capable of relating to it. They were no more capable of relating to me than relating to the men who returned from Vietnam—men whose boundaries had been blown away by a land mine in Da Nang, by machine guns surrounding Dak To, or by a sadistic guard in Hoa Lo prison.

My pain did not begin to compare with the pain of those men. But the explosion of my boundaries was the same, and the results of that explosion on those around me had the same effect as on the families of Vietnam veterans.

People want to deny that Vietnam ever happened. People want to deny that sexual abuse of children exists. To accept that these horrendous things occur means having to look inward at one's own pain, at one's *own* need for healing—a frightening prospect.

How does healing begin? Does one go to therapy for a few hours, weeks, months, years? After that, is one completely well? How do you judge when someone is emotionally well? Who sets the standards? Too often the standard states: Anyone inside my type of boundary is well. Anyone with boundaries different from mine is ill.

Many of the people around me did not understand that seven months of intensive therapy could not entirely erase my Sobbing Hurting Child. My time in therapy uncovered that child and helped me realize how hard she had fought to let me know she existed. Therapy gave me ways to deal with that child, but the child could not be erased. Not again.

Some people thought that was the purpose of therapy: to make the pain disappear. They did not realize that healing is a lifelong journey, that some wounds are never completely repaired. One can find the necessary care to close the open wounds, but scars always remain. The body can again function in what seems to be a normal capacity, but the skin is taut and sensitive to touch, like a person with severe burns all over her body. Fire has a way of touching and searing all the way to the soul. So it is with sexual abuse. It is a fire that burns. For some, the deep burns are only partial. For me, the burns covered my whole being.

I was not certain what to do with my Sobbing Hurting Child. I did not know whether to let people know that the little girl was always there, bleeding with pain, or to tell them everything was fine. Saying everything was fine was a lie, but no one wanted to hear the pain.

Todd and I continued to see Dr. Earle but the schedule of our sessions was often sporadic. Despite the problems in our counseling sessions we kept up our public image of the perfect, happy, church-going couple. We attended and hosted din-

ners and art shows, all with smiles and kind words
to each other. In private, I experienced our communication as minimal with angry silences filling the
house.

Thoughts of Burlingame brought peace and long-
ing into my heart. I thought of the long quiet walks
I took on Saturdays, building up the strength of my
legs. I loved being outside, seeing the trees and
flowers. There was nothing to disturb the peace
and quiet—no conflicts involving husband,
mother, relatives, friends, church people, work, gallery, broken promises, bad deals and trades, and on
and on. In Scottsdale, it was not okay to be me, to
enjoy the beauty, to laugh and talk without thinking about what I should or should not say.

I attended church regularly. I loved the people
who supported me in prayer while I was in therapy.
I appreciated those who had sent letters and cards
of encouragement. Without all of them, I couldn't
have made it through the seven months of therapy.
It was their love, their support, that saw me
through.

Occasionally people at church would quietly slip
up to me and give me a hug. The tears in their eyes
said, "I understand, I've been there too." I so
wanted to reach out and say, "It's okay to let that
Sobbing Child come out. It's safe now. God made
you and He didn't intend for you to stay bound—
imprisoned."

The God in whom I now believed saw each
human being—male or female, child or adult,
white or nonwhite—as an equal, as a beloved person, a person of worth and value, a person with a
right to be free. The God I was learning to trust and

to love was not a God who taught that women and children and people of nonwhite races were second-class citizens.

The God who had kept me alive through the terror of my attack, who had kept me alive through the pain of my therapy, surely did not plan to allow me to die now. Each day I became more certain that God was happy with the Feeling Adult who was continuing to grow within me. My Feeling Adult questioned and tested, trying to determine her own values and beliefs, even though some ran contrary to the beliefs of those she loved.

I no longer saw myself as just a woman. I had begun to believe in my freedom as a person—a separate person, with my own opinions and needs, who believed in the rightness of meeting those needs.

I felt somehow humankind's interpretations had distorted what God had originally intended. Surely God did not intend His church to squash the persons He had created us to be.

My old fears of making a mistake created a bitter battle against my fulfillment of my needs. In my unconscious, making a mistake meant getting wiped out. Making a mistake meant missing my bus stop and being physically and sexually attacked to the point of annihilation. All my life since the attack, I had made my choices with a life or death intensity.

The battle raged on in my mind. I was lonely and afraid. I did not know what was right or wrong at times. But I knew instinctively that this person inside me was precious and God-given and God-ordained to have life.

My headaches increased to the same level of pain as before I left for Burlingame. New stresses poured in from every side, pushing me deeper into the quicksand and mire.

I began to recognize and take responsibility for the things I had done that had contributed to the problems in our marriage. Todd was always more compassionate, more emotional, than I was. He had been a "feeling" person when we married. The Controlling Child part of me was threatened by feelings, so gradually I had ignored, pushed down, dominated, and manipulated Todd's Original Child, until that child had almost disappeared.

We had truly loved each other. If only we had known it was okay to feel. Okay to take care of ourselves. Okay to be two separate people joined in a mutually rewarding, mutually nuturing relationship.

I hoped and I prayed that that could still happen. What if it didn't? Divorce was not an option for me.

In my growth, I saw that the extreme of submission is when "self" is completely lost to others. The extreme of humanism is when self is pushed to power at the expense of others. I now felt that a genuinely spiritual person is one who has a balance between the two. A person who recognizes God in his or her life, but who also has a clear perception of his or her own worth. When one is able to take care of one's self and one's own needs, then one can choose to extend one's self and reach out to care for others in a giving, loving way.

Hesitantly, I approached Dr. Earle with my school plans. I gave him a brief sketch, outlining my plans for eventually getting my doctorate and also doing public speaking. "This is what I would like to do. But it all depends on how I resolve the issues in my marriage."

Dr. Earle responded, "This may be exactly what you've needed, Marilyn. You have the intellect, talent, experience, and skills to do these things. You go right on and do the very best you can. Learn, speak, travel, be useful in other people's lives; be yourself."

Dr. Earle urged me to get in touch with what I felt, with what I wanted. What about school?

I struggled with my response. "I've never had a goal for myself since I've been married. My goals have always been for Todd, for my family, for my church, for MORE THAN FRIENDS. Never for me." I took a deep breath. "Going back to school would be the first goal I've had for myself in twenty-six years."

Dr. Earle smiled broadly. "And it's a good goal too. Go for it!"

Pleased by Dr. Earle's (and Dr. Danylchuk's) encouragement, I began the next segment of my school goals. I scrounged through boxes and files, finding the documents I needed to gain school credits for work I had already done. I filled three large notebooks with documents from all my years of work, dating back to my first job in Prescott with Jack Mims. I smiled, glad for once that as a pack rat I never threw anything away. The excitement of finally reaching for something I wanted to do exceeded the difficulty of finding and putting together photos, newspaper articles, and typewritten verifications of my past experience. My school advisor helped me choose the strongest documentation.

I received credit for courses in marketing as a result of all my work in retailing; for my work in MORE THAN FRIENDS, I received credits for courses in psychology. Excitedly, I scheduled the balance of my classes and packed my days with studying. I was well on my way.

And then, a new joy arrived to extend the family's happiness. Janell Joy was born to Jinger and Brad, making B.J. a proud older brother.

The joy mingled with the battles.

My Original Feeling Child felt invigorated by the excitement and challenge of school. She felt invigorated by my increasing physical strength despite my recurring headaches and body pain.

I was now thin, trim, and tan. Jinger and Missy teased me about my nongrandmotherly image in my new bikini. I was attending strenuous aerobic sessions with Missy and loving it.

Both Jinger and Missy were professional models. They taught me new ways to do my hair and makeup. They encouraged me to shop for clothes that my Original Feeling Child would enjoy. My Controlling Child had worn only tan, brown, black, and navy. My Original Child loved pink and lavender, and wearing lacy lingerie, silky soft fabrics, swirling skirts—not just ultra-suede business suits.

Jinger and Missy were delighted by my regenerated size-six figure, the same as theirs. They decided Mom's closet was the best boutique in town. My new, relaxed relationship with my daughters was wonderful for all three of us. We were relating as friends, as equals. I was starting to be real.

My time with my family, with Dr. Earle, with Cynthia, and with my MORE THAN FRIENDS group, my time at school, and occasional follow-up times with Dr. Danylchuk helped pull me out of the swamp long enough to breathe, to gain strength.

There continued to be times of extreme joy one hour, followed by an hour or two of tremendous, screaming frustration. Sadness, fear, humiliation, pain, peace, contentment, and growth could all squeeze themselves into a single day. Slowly, it seemed the joys were making progress on the frustrations. Only looking back could anyone see that change. The swamp was drying up, if only an inch at a time.

The essence of the person called "Marilyn" had begun to travel farther and farther into her own frontier. Step by step, she left the old boundaries behind—the boundaries of her generation, her culture, her heritage.

To return to those old boundaries meant burying her Original Feeling Child once again. But she had held that Child, touched that Child, felt that Child, and of one thing she was certain: once you have really touched into your Original Feeling Child, you will never be content to lose that child ever again.

But at what price to capture the essence of one's true self? Divorce? Loss of family, friends, reputation, financial security? I did not want to begin to consider the cost.

◆ 12 ◆

Hunks of Clay

Standing on a hill overlooking my frontier, I could see a valley below me, flowers, trees, green grass, streams—streams of knowledge. For me, Ottawa University had become literally an oasis in the Arizona desert.

My Original Child believed that to have vast intellectual knowledge is admirable, but to have an understanding of the heart and soul is far preferable. To become intimately acquainted with all three became an impelling aspiration for me.

I searched for intellectual knowledge so that I could understand and help other hurting hearts and souls. I did not want intellectual knowledge that would take me away from the God I loved, but knowledge that would help me understand His universe, and the people in it, more fully.

My search for an appropriate master's program began shortly after I started my B.A. program. I still had not lost my need to cover every base and plan ahead. As I looked for a graduate school, Dr. Earle suggested I see his friend, Dr. Sandy Mazen, a professor in the counseling department at Arizona State University.

To my disappointment, Dr. Mazen encouraged me to look for a program elsewhere. "The psychology program here is for someone who can fit into this mold. You already have a specific field in which you are becoming an expert. Because of your age, you don't want to waste a lot of time in extraneous information."

He paused, tilted his head, and looked at me. "Would you consider talking to my graduate students about your therapy experience?"

My disappointment faded. "I'd love to talk about regression that works.' There have been so many negative experiences with improperly handled regressive therapy."

Dr. Mazen stroked his mustache. "I can't get away from feeling that you could help me in my other work, too."

"And what work is that?"

"I do group and individual therapy with rapists and child molesters at the Arizona State Prison in Florence."

I caught my breath. "Really?" My heart jumped. My frightened inner children screeched, "Go back to a *prison*? And with *offenders*?!"

But my Feeling Adult answered Dr. Mazen. "One of the reasons I share my story publicly is because many offenders feel the victim wasn't 're-ally hurt' and would 'forget' the incident." I paused. "I have a tape of one of my sessions where I relive the attack. I don't think I'm ready to go into a prison personally, but maybe the tape would help."

Dr. Mazen looked pensive, his hand covering his mouth, his eyes focusing on nothing in particular. After a moment, he seemed to come back to our conversation. "I'm sitting here fantasizing what the reaction would be if I played that tape for my group at the prison."

I let my thoughts join his. "Maybe that would help. Many times a sexual assault victim is unable to scream. And even if the victim does scream, perhaps the offender is so preoccupied he can't absorb it."

Dr. Mazen leaned toward me. "Marilyn, the men I work with are genuinely trying to change. I think your tape could have a profound impact on them."

I left the office, hearing Dr. Mazen's last words as he said goodbye: "I firmly believe there are 'no accidents.' I'm looking forward to seeing more of you."

I continued to attend classes, studying in spite of my continuing headaches and body pain. My favorite class, Counseling Theories, was taught by Dr. George Larsen. I took copious notes and nodded a lot. This man taught things I wished the rest of the world could hear.

Dr. Larsen strolled across the front of the class, speaking with a calm authority. "To ignore a client's past, if that past contains physical and/or emotional abuse, and use behavior modification only is ineffectual and futile."

I cheered silently at this simple statement of vital importance. Dr. Larsen seemed truly to understand the heart of therapy.

One evening after class, he approached me as I closed my notebook. "Would you like to go for coffee? I have a client I'd like to discuss with you."

I readily agreed, flattered to think my teacher would request my help.

His client, Nancy, had been the victim of severe abuse, both sexual and emotional. Often suicidal, she had been hospitalized in a psychiatric ward numerous times.

As I listened to Dr. Larsen reveal the details, I thought through my own painful months in therapy. Searching the memories, I found an experience similar to what he described. I discussed with him what had been most beneficial and healing for me at the time.

The next week over coffee, Dr. Larsen expressed his pleasure at the results of my suggestion. He asked for my opinion a second time, and I again replied from my own experience.

As the weeks passed, I discovered my therapy was not only healing for me, but was also becoming the genesis of therapeutic information that could be beneficial for others.

The final class assignment challenged me to examine my therapy to determine the various theoretical concepts my therapist used in treatment.

At home, I took large easel sheets and spread them all over my office floor, making diagrams of my seven months in Burlingame. One night, the thoughts and processes stirred my mind to action rather than sleep. I heeded the prompting, got out of bed in the middle of the night, and worked until dawn.

I scribbled diagrams, circles, triangles, and outlines across the easel pages as ideas poured forth from some hidden well. In the daylight, huge sheets of paper lay strewn about like the fragments of a giant's journal, a journal bleeding its story in slashes and splashes of colored ink.

As I studied the chaos, I noticed an emerging pattern. For days, the work totally obsessed me. Many times I filled a legal pad with notes and sketches in one sitting. The notes and diagrams led to new thoughts as I attempted to find something visual to present to the class that would illustrate the concept of a "pool of pain."

The night of my presentation, I told the story of my seven months in therapy. Then I placed five bottles of graduated sizes, each filled with colored water varying from light to dark, on the table in front of me. I took a deep breath and began.

"Many people have asked why I stayed in therapy so long. Why couldn't I return home right after my 'volcano'? Wasn't cognition enough?

"Perhaps these bottles, representing pools of pain, will show you why I chose to remain in therapy. How long a person stays in treatment is determined, in part, by the size and intensity of his or her 'pool of pain.'"

I reached for the smallest bottle and held it up for the class to see. The water was not clear; it was tinged with brown. "This bottle represents a girl whose mother and father loved her very much. However, she had an older brother who constantly picked on her. Her pool of pain is not too large and has a lid which can be removed fairly easily to allow her to deal with her past."

The next bottle I held in my hand was slightly larger and slightly darker. "This bottle represents a boy whose mother was loving but his father was not. His dad constantly berated him, telling him he was stupid, and hassled him for bringing home B's instead of A's and for not making first string in football. This pool of pain is darker, but it also has a lid which can be removed.

"The third one is a child whose mother and father were both very unloving. They never picked him up, hugged him, or told him he was loved. Fortunately, he had a wonderful grandmother who spent time with him baking cookies and reading him stories."

The fourth bottle was very tall and darkly tinged with brown. There was no clarity in this bottle at all. It was a shade short of being completely black. "This bottle is a child of incest. She has a pool of pain that is deep and enormous. Instead of a lid, she has a cork pushed in the opening, which is difficult to remove. She has buried many of the memories and most of the feelings surrounding her painful childhood."

I placed the fourth bottle on the table. I sucked in my breath ever so slightly as I picked up the fifth bottle. The class had grasped the concept so well that, as they looked at the ugly bottle, their facial expressions reflected the pain the bottle represented. The water, like blackened slime, was held in by a cork shoved all the way down into the opening.

My hands trembled as I spoke. "The last bottle is me, with a dark, rumbling pool of pain, increasing daily in intensity. Any glass bottle, with pressure building inside, will eventually burst, exploding into fragments if the pressure is not released. Human beings shatter differently, but in ways that are equally destructive. Some develop addictive behaviors, becoming offenders to themselves and sometimes to others. Some become damaged emotionally. Others, like myself, develop physiological symptoms."

I picked up pieces of clay and began to stick them onto the bottle. "As I apply these bits of clay, I want you to visualize how my body responded to my repressed memories and feelings. My unconscious used my body in an attempt to tell my conscious about my attack. Since my body could not explode like a bottle, it released its inner pain in ways that were *duplications* of the assault."

I then listed my physiological symptoms: leg aches, headaches, chest pains, jaw trouble, asthma, constant phlegm in my throat. I reached under the table to bring out another bottle: a large bottle, completely covered with hunks of clay, which I had sprayed with black paint.

"This ugly bottle is me, the way I looked the day I arrived in Burlingame—a giant lumpy mass of physical and emotional pain. You will note that this bottle has a cork rammed deeply inside, making it impossible to remove by hand without special help."

I picked up a wine-bottle opener. "This corkscrew represents the help I received—regressive therapy. The therapy I received loosened that cork so the pain building within the bottle could be released before it exploded into suicide or physiological and/or emotional damage beyond repair.

"We have all seen a champagne bottle opened—the cork flies and champagne spews forth from the release of pressure. But when the foam dies down, the bottle is still basically full. The night my volcano blew, my cork exploded from my bottle. Some of the pain came with it. But my bottle, containing the giant pool of pain, was still nearly full. Just knowing about the attack did not make me well. Cognition alone was not enough. I then had to begin the long, difficult process of pouring out that pain."

A classmate raised her hand. "How can you do that?"

"It can be done two ways. One is to turn the bottle upside down, dumping out all of the poison at once. To do so would be tantamount to a massive nervous breakdown, in which recovery takes a long time and may never be completed."

From under the table, I retrieved a bottle filled with blue colored water and a bottle of oil. "The other method of removing pain is by adding to the bottle something heavier than the pain. The bottle of colored water is my therapist, and the oil represents me."

I held the two bottles high and began to add the water to the oil. "This is what my therapist did for me. He came in, went under, and supported me. His caring became heavier than my pain, allowing my pain to be released a little at a time."

I smiled at the group and went on. "In my opinion, no one ever completely empties out the pain. No matter how often you wash an oily bottle, it still retains a residue of oil."

I set down the bottles and leaned forward toward the audience. "My healing was a three-fold process: first, removing the cork, which represented my Controlling Child who held down my painful memories and feelings; second, releasing the pain of my Sobbing Hurting Child within that pool; and third, refilling the bottle by restoring my Original Feeling Child, the child I was created to be."

Dr. Larsen threw me a smile and a big "Okay" sign. I returned the smile. Sharing my story with lay persons was one thing. Presenting a theory to an academic group was entirely different. Yet I survived and even received positive comments from my classmates.

A week later, I gave my presentation to Dr. Mazon's graduate students in counseling psychology at Arizona State University. As I finished, I asked for questions.

Suddenly, a scream split the quiet. Donna, one of the students, writhed in her chair, her body contorting into the familiar posture of an abuse victim.

Instantly, I was beside her, easing her onto the floor. Cradling her in my arms, I whispered softly, "I'm here, just let it come. I'll take care of you."

Sobbing, screaming, whimpering, Donna became a five-year-old taken into a basement and molested. As I worked with her, Donna uncovered three totally repressed sexual assaults.

The students were mesmerized. They hardly expected Donna to crumble into her past. They knew her as a therapist, working on her second master's degree. Some knew she had been in and out of therapy for more than twenty years. They gradually slipped away, going on to their other classes, unaware that this was the first "client" I had ever worked with.

Several hours passed before Donna could sit up, feeling released and greatly surprised by what had occurred. She wiped her eyes and looked at me. "I've always known there was something more I needed to work on and never have been able to touch it. But today, as I listened to you, it was as though something inside me leapt out to touch you. Somehow I knew you would know who I am. At last it was safe to come out from where I've been buried for more than fifty years."

I shared my experience with Dr. Larsen one Saturday afternoon. Our coffee sessions had expanded to include Saturdays in my office at home, going over my charts.

That day he shook his head as he gazed at the charts. "You know, Marilyn, even though I have a doctorate and two master's degrees, I've never received specialized training on how to treat a victim of sexual abuse." He flipped through a few charts and stopped. "I feel most theory is written by theorists and therapists standing on the outside looking in, trying to figure out what's going on in the mind of the child."

I replied, "But I *am* that child. I'm standing on the inside looking out. I can tell you what that child feels and some of what you, as a therapist, can do to help that child become well. A doctor can't prescribe an antidote unless he knows the name of the poison. Think how much more effective therapists could be if they understood what happens in the unconscious mind of a child in times of trauma and/or deprivation."

"Well, your concepts certainly have been helpful with Nancy. Her growth progressed more quickly with your help."

Excitement caught my voice and carried my thoughts rapidly to Dr. Larsen. "I've been doing a lot of research on this process of 'splitting'—the *normal* defense mechanism that activates in times of trauma and deprivation. There's so much confusion surrounding it. People get it mixed up with schizophrenia. As you know, *schizoid* is Greek for *split*."

I handed him a rough draft of my graduation mini-thesis (he was on my committee) and continued, "After a lot of study and deliberation, I've decided to use the word *scindo*, Latin for *split*, to describe this innate emotional defense system. I'm calling my theory the Scindo Syndrome.

His eyes reflected his approval as I continued, "I feel there's a definite pattern to a child's responses to trauma and/or deprivation—the things that make it necessary for that child to 'split' in order to survive. That's what these charts are all about."

I grinned as I said, "George, I'm still basically a salesperson at heart. Now, instead of selling Levi's, boots, or western art, I'm trying to sell people on the concept that it's okay to seek therapeutic help. And to sell therapists on being prepared to provide that help."

He nodded, "That's why you're such a help with Nancy. I'm just beginning to realize she's a multiple personality. I used to think multiplicity was rare. But after listening to you, I think it's more common than most people realize."

George leaned over and studied the easel sheets now strewn all over the office floor. "If these charts are correct, it appears that *every* person is at least a 'multiple of three.'"

"So you think my theory will help people?"

Dr. Larsen immediately responded, "I think you're going to be pleasantly surprised to find how applicable it really is." With Dr. Larsen's encouragement, I was beginning to accept the idea that my theories might be useful to other people.

Two years had passed since I left for therapy. Could it possibly have been that long?

The year 1982 closed with my compass tipping toward a direction I could not comprehend. The new year of 1983 took me by the hand and pointed a path leading far into the future, a future with bright new possibilities. Speaking engagements began to fill my calendar.

In January, I flew to Austin, Texas, to meet Florence Littauer for another CLASS presentation. I arrived in Texas two days before my presentation so I could interview therapists in the Austin area. I wanted to have counselors to whom I could refer the many hurting women who surrounded me after my talks.

I also stayed three days after the seminar, counseling twelve to fifteen hours a day. The same comments poured out from each woman. "I never told anyone this before." Or "I told my pastor (doctor, counselor, teacher) and he said it was 'no big deal' and not to deal with it." Or "I was told if I would only increase my Bible reading and prayer time to become more spiritual, then I would become well. I've tried and tried to do that. So why do I still hurt so much?"

My heart ached with the pain pouring out before me. My Sobbing Child stomped her feet in rage. "Sexual abuse *is* a big deal!"

I explained to the women that it is not just sexual abuse that hurts. Any type of physical or emotional abuse is devastating to a child. Over and over I told them that it is right to seek therapy for emotional pain and that it is not unspiritual to do so.

I began receiving phone calls and letters from people who told me that my presentation had been a life saving experience for them. As I discussed these comments with Todd, I sensed his confusion. I felt he was struggling with his concern for these hurting people and yet I also felt that he experienced my work as causing us to drift farther apart.

I thought about what Todd and I had been together and what we could become. We had made a great team as business partners. Each knew what to say and when to say it. Always warm, friendly, and helpful, Todd had an incredible ability for creating a unique atmosphere for a store or gallery, and he was a great salesman. I was a good business administrator, and I could also sell. Together we created fascinating art shows. *But an intimate relationship? Did we ever have the skills to create that?*

Would there really be a chance for Todd and me? Was a close intimate relationship really possible for us? Could I be tolerant of his needs? Would he be supportive of me? Somehow I felt that an intimate relationship, physically and emotionally, simply might never happen for me.

I knew that life walking on my frontier was now terribly lonely, but my life within anyone else's boundaries, including my husband's, had been even more lonely. I had wanted to walk the path together. It was not happening that way. Was I selfish? Maybe. I loved school. I loved seeing lives changed because of my work.

♦ 13 ♦

The Razor Wire Fence

Some of my old support system grew apathetic and then antagonistic. Many of my church friends disagreed with my independence and my goals that did not focus on my husband.

My parents were confused about what happened to me so many years ago and what I was doing now. Their generation never spoke publicly of their pain; they simply endured in silence.

Jinger and Missy didn't want to take sides. They loved and supported both Todd and me. They were angry at each of us for our part in the unraveling of the marriage.

I no longer knew whether I loved him or not. I was tired. I really did not know if I wanted to struggle with our problems, or him, anymore. The tension and stress had increased my physical pain. Working on the never-ending stack of gallery ledgers often required strapping a heating pad around me to alleviate the severe ache in my chest.

My sense of sanity and balance often depended upon my therapy sessions with Dr. Earle. I still visited Burlingame to see Dr. Danylchuk. Now, however, he was advising me on my theoretical studies.

His knowledge of the defense mechanism of splitting, the subject of his graduate thesis, added to my understanding of this process. During these days I became more excited as we discussed new insights and ideas. With each discussion my theory expanded.

My Original Feeling Child loved school and exploring new vistas. One of my primary goals was to let her continue to grow in all areas. She had been in solitary confinement for thirty-six years! Now she was running over fields, climbing trees, and wading barefoot in streams. I could never imprison her again.

As she ran, I discovered I wasn't so alone anymore. A new wider support system was emerging.

In June 1983, Missy graduated with honors from Westmont College in Santa Barbara, California. Our entire family attended, glad to share in the pride of her accomplishments. Then it was my turn to graduate, also with honors from Ottawa University with a Bachelor's Degree in Psychology. Everyone attended my graduation—everyone except Todd, who had gone on a fishing trip.

I began working at the Center Against Sexual Assault (CASA) in Phoenix to fulfill the internship requirement for my master's degree in psychology from California State University at Sonoma. Carol Fowler, the director of the center, and Jeff Kirkendall, one of the center's therapists, took time to share their knowledge of the many aspects of victimization. There was still much I needed to learn.

At the center, I answered the hot line, worked with adolescent incest victims and rape victims, and helped adults molested as children. I counseled individuals and assisted in groups. The problems I encountered overwhelmed me. What should one do with two little girls ages three and five who are brought in with gonorrhea of the mouth? How do you begin to treat a thirteen-year-old who has had sex for nine years?

I looked forward to being a co-therapist for a women's group. The first night, I noticed a woman named Virginia huddled in the corner, withdrawn and visibly shaking. I asked each woman to share her goals. Virginia kept her head down as she shared that her goal was "to die." She had been hospitalized for asthma thirty-two times.

I brought my easel pad to the second session and drew a picture of the steel box where I had buried my Sobbing Hurting Child after the attack. I encouraged the other women to also draw pictures of their Sobbing Child's hiding place. Each one immediately knew the place and the feelings of that hidden child. No one expected Virginia to share, yet she uncurled herself from the corner long enough to give a detailed description of her own Sobbing Child.

At the end of the evening, Virginia approached me. In a whispery voice, she said to the floor, "I . . . I think I could use some extra help. You are the first person who seems to know what's going on inside me. Would you be willing to see me privately every week?"

I pulled Virginia close and gave her a big hug. "I'd love to spend more time with you, Virginia."

During our individiual sessions, Virginia revealed her artistic talent. She captured my concept of the "children" on paper, portraying them as fascinating little creatures who had no age, sex, or race, and no features—only pure emotion. The Sobbing Hurting Child had an anchor pulling the terrified child off a cliff; the Original Feeling Child happily flew a kite with an anchor on it; and the Controlling Child stood defiantly, with hands on hips, upon a tightly locked box.

As the months passed, Virginia's feelings of self-esteem gained in strength. As a result of her artwork, her Original Child emerged and bloomed, expressing joy in discovering the child she was created to be.

As I tried to transfer my knowledge of my own inner children to Virginia, my first "real client," I learned and I grew. Each question she asked tested my knowledge. Sometimes the answers came from my own children inside. Many times I raced for my textbooks; questioned Carol, Jeff, the other counselors; or simply said, "I don't know."

I often was overzealous, like a new convert to religion or abstinence. I wanted to change the world NOW. I made dogmatic statements. I did not always listen. I sometimes thought I knew more about the unconscious than anyone else. I did not.

Yet daily, I found my Feeling Adult was becoming more present. At first I thought she was simply my Original Feeling Child, grown up. But my Feeling Adult was a lot more.

In my therapy, I had worked long and hard to start to release the negative parts of my Controlling Child and my Sobbing Hurting Child. I still had more of that work ahead of me, but I began to considered their *positive* values.

My Controlling Child had served me well for many years, helping me to be an excellent organizer, a good administrator, a clear thinker, and an enthusiastic teacher. She now helped me to set healthy boundaries and was also my protector in times of trauma. I did not want to lose her.

My Sobbing Hurting Child gave me empathy and compassion. She could look in Virginia's eyes, or Donna's, or Linda's, and know almost immediately what she felt, how deeply she hurt, how lonely and afraid she was.

Both my Controlling Child and my Sobbing Hurting Child had been created out of my Original Feeling Child. It was now time to allow them to reunite—to return with the combination of their experiences, knowledge, and feelings. Together, the three children began to mature and were slowly growing into a true Feeling Adult—an adult with the capacity to express all emotions—to feel joy, anger, and pain, but in an appropriate way.

The whole had become greater than the sum of the parts. This concept became the essence of my Scindo Syndrome Theory. As I worked and studied, as I read case studies and attended CLASS seminars, I learned a startling and haunting fact. I shook my head over and over, not wanting to believe it was true. *Sexual abuse seems to be more prevalent in strongly religious homes.*

My speaking engagements were verifying this. After speaking to church groups, many women told me of abuse by a family member who was a pastor, deacon, or Sunday-school teacher. When I urged them to seek therapy, the victims often told me they could not because the offender was still active in a church position. They did not want to ruin his reputation, and they feared they would not be believed.

At first, Florence Littauer shook her head in disbelief when I told her this, but watching the women pour down the aisles after my CLASS presentations changed her mind.

Our anger boiled when talking to numerous pastors about this problem. Several responded by telling us not to discuss this publicly. They did not want us to give the "world" something else to criticize the church about.

I once retorted, "How ridiculous! If we don't police our own ranks, who will? Abuse, particularly incest, breeds in silence. It will never be stopped until we bring it out, into the open, and deal with it."

I decided if something could be done to change those insidious patterns, wherever they were found, I wanted to be a part of that change—with my talks, my theory, and my tape.

The tape I had mentioned to Dr. Mazen became one of the tools to begin that change. It is a twenty-minute cassette tape of one of my regressive therapy sessions in Burlingame. It brings anyone who listens to it agonizingly close to the torment of a child in the midst of incredible terror.

Carol Fowler used the tape in a session with incest offenders at the CASA. She told me that during the twenty minutes it played, the offenders cried, beat the walls, and dropped deeply into their own pain. They became willing to talk about their own abuse experiences.

Carol said offenders often depersonalized their

victims. She suggested I find some photos of my child to show while the men listened to the tape.

I scoured my childhood photo album and chose forty pictures from infancy to adulthood. Until age eight, all the photos showed me with bright eyes and a wide open smile. But at nine, the smile faded and a sadness permeated my eyes, becoming a window on my pain. Through elementary school and junior high, the closed-mouth smile dominated the photographs. In high school, the smile returned, but the eyes still showed the pain of my Sobbing Child.

I had slides made of the photos. I synchronized the slides with the tape, thus putting a face with the terror and horror of the attack.

I was asked to use the presentation the following week. Dr. Paul Duda, the resident psychologist at the Adobe Mountain Juvenile Institution, asked if I would speak to his group of teenage offenders. My Sobbing Hurting Child instantly reminded me of her frightened reaction to Dr. Mazen's invitation to the adult prison at Florence.

I hesitantly agreed to go to Adobe. I had a difficult time speaking to "safe, normal" people. Could I hold myself together to speak to a group of rapists and child molesters? In a prison?

A knot twisted in my stomach as I approached the towering fence with a razor wire ribbon around the top. I waited as the television camera scanned my face. The huge gate slowly swung open. I stepped through and crossed the forty-foot "no man's land" toward the second fence, a twin to the first. Again, I waited as a camera lens scanned me, then I was allowed to enter. As I heard the gate close, I remembered being told by a friend who was a corrections official that many people do not feel comfortable working in a prison. "There's something about having that gate slam shut *behind* you."

As I walked across the immaculately groomed lawn toward the main building, I noticed groups of young boys gardening. *They're just kids. What happened to them! What would make them do something so terrible that they would end up here!*

Dr. Duda had given me a list of the boys and their offenses: four rapists and three child molesters, with a long list of victims. As I read through the list again, my Sobbing Child gulped, struggling with her own feelings as a victim. I was about to face known rapists for the first time.

I stood stiff and uncomfortable at the front of the room, trying to act relaxed as the boys filed into the room. Dr. Duda and two counselors spaced themselves between the boys as I began my presentation.

"I know you must be wondering what I'm doing here. I'm here for two reasons. First, I'm here to help you realize the enormity of the pain you caused your victims."

I looked around the room at the young faces staring back at me. Defiance was clear in their faces and bodies as they slumped in their chairs with their arms crossed over their chests. They obviously did not want to listen to me.

"Second, I'm here to help you start to get in touch with your own pain. I know that the majority of sex offenders have themselves been victims of sexual abuse and that all of you have been the recipients of emotional and physical abuse. Consequently, I come to you today, not as victim to offender, but as victim to victim."

The boys shifted uneasily in their chairs as I began, "No, not me! I had a perfect childhood."

My voice continued while my mind concentrated on each youthful offender. I tried to let my Sobbing Hurting Child reach out to coax the hurting child out of each boy.

At the end of my talk, I reached for the tape, explaining to the boys what they would see and hear next. I felt they would have all dashed for the nearest exit if Dr. Duda and his staff were not positioned solidly between them.

I started the projector and turned on the recorder, frantically praying, *Lord, please help me get through this. I'm not sure I can make it alone. Oh God, I'm so afraid!*

A smiling, dark-haired baby flashed onto the screen as a hysterical scream split the silence. Each body in the room tensed and shuddered, as audible gasps escaped from tightly clenched teeth.

The screams stopped momentarily as a terror-filled voice filled the air. "Not me! Not me! Please don't hurt me anymore!"

The horrible pain of all children molested, hit, and otherwise abused, permeated the room—a common pain, intense, scathing, destructive, a pain that has to be denied to be coped with. The boys all knew the sound of that pain. They had felt it themselves.

Gradually, each boy reached into his own blackness, opened his deep pool of pain, and allowed his own Sobbing Hurting Child to venture forth, some for the very first time.

Brian's arrogant, swaggering attitude crumbled and his voice broke as he struggled through his story of being the victim of repeated sexual abuse by his father. Unable to release his anger at his father without being beaten, Brian had vented his hostility by raping.

Jerry's rage rumbled against his father who came home drunk nearly every night and hauled his children and wife out, one by one, to beat them severely, sometimes with a baseball bat. The bitterness in Jerry's eyes erupted into tears as he spoke. "That tape sounded just like my mom and my sisters as my dad beat them. I used to try so hard to stop him, but I was too little. When I did, he'd knock me senseless. I felt so helpless and powerless!"

Like Brian, Jerry had also been imprisoned for rape, trying to regain the lost sense of control and power by abusing someone weaker, younger, or smaller than him.

Chuck quietly stated that he had had a normal family life and parents who were good to him. Dr. Duda gently probed deeper into the past of this small thirteen-year-old who had been arrested for forcing a younger boy into oral copulation at knifepoint. Chuck finally spoke of a time when his father had had too much to drink and had thrown eight-year-old Chuck down the stairs, breaking his arm. The sadistic father stood laughing at the top of the stairwell, refusing for several hours to let Chuck's mother take him to the doctor. The astounded responses of the group helped Chuck realize that *this was abuse.*

Another boy told of how he was often left alone for days without care or food. The stories of horror continued through the passing hours.

My attack had terrorized me as a child, but my abuse happened only once, and I had loving, caring parents. I knew my attack was not the worst thing that ever happened to a child. The stories these boys told emphasized that. It no longer seemed to matter to me that they had responded to that hurt by hurting others. Their abuse of others was wrong. I did not condone it, but now I understood.

That day, when I looked at each boy, I looked inside and saw a terrified, lonely, abused child. I saw how he had become an angry, abusive person; with some, I was amazed that the rage had not led to murder.

I knew I was already touching the lives of many women who had been abused as children. Working with victims was difficult work, but working with offenders? Was I willing to chose to do that? Perhaps these boys could relate to my pain and see that I related to theirs. Perhaps they might see that healing, no matter how slight, might be possible for them, too.

Most of all I wanted them to know that they were not the trash, scum, and filth that they all perceived themselves to be. Somehow I wanted to help them see that buried underneath that mound of trash was a valuable child—a child that God could see, a child that I saw in each one of them that day, upon my first return to prison.

At the end of the long day, I looked around at the

boys. Our circle had become smaller, their chairs edged in closer to me. "You've all become very special to me today. It means a lot that each of you has been willing to share so deeply and honestly."

I smiled as I stood up. "Since I don't receive any pay for my work, do you think I could get paid with a hug from each of you?"

Shoulders sagging, heads down, anger and rebellion gone, they were just boys—deeply hurting boys. Most fought back tears. I reached out to Chuck. He clung to me and sobbed.

My tears flowed, too, as I exclaimed silently, *But he's so little! O dear God, how can this happen?!*

Driving home past the elegant homes of Paradise Valley, I wanted to scream, *Do you people know what's happening this very instant to thousands of children? Do you give a damn that they are being beaten and abused? Well, you'd better. Because one day, one of those abused children is going to abuse one of yours.*

I shook my head as I approached my own beautiful house. *I wonder how Todd would react if he knew I just left a part of my heart with those boys at Adobe? Not just boys, but rapists and child molesters.* So I did not tell him. I walked on, leaving him farther and farther behind me.

I took my newfound interest in prison work to my master's research. What creates a sex offender? I could not view them as "faceless monsters" or "slobbering old men in trench coats" any more. I watched incest offenders coming to the CASA for Carol and Jeff's therapy group: an engineer, an architect, a pastor, a computer analyst, a mechanic, a politician, and a teacher. They were not the scum of the earth. They were human beings with a dark side no one wanted to admit.

I questioned my mentors. I read. I researched. Statistics on sexual abuse were just beginning to surface, and they changed daily. Some figures stated that about 20 percent of all sex offenses are the crimes mentioned most often in the newspapers: the ones committed by the sociopath, the psychopath, those into satanic ritual abuse—offenders who mutilate, kill, or horribly abuse their victims. However, the general public tends to lump all sex offenders in this same category.

True, all abuse is terribly damaging to the victim. No one was denying that. But stopping the abuse? How? Where did one begin?

For some of us, part of the answer means working with the remaining 80 percent of offenders who are capable of change. Change is possible if trained therapists are available and if the offenders are willing to do the incredibly painful work that true change demands.

Dr. Mazen told me that without treatment, over 85 percent of sex offenders will re-offend upon release from prison. The Sex Offender Treatment Program (SOTP), which he had started at the state prison in Florence, had drastically reduced recidivism.

Taxpayers cannot begin to bear the burden of keeping all sex offenders imprisoned for a lifetime. It was becoming a difficult choice: pay the price of more and more prisons and still have a horrendous recidivism rate which produces more victims, or *provide therapy*.

In Arizona, Dr. Sandy Mazen was one of the

pioneers on this frightening frontier. Dr. Mazen, Dr. Duda, Carol, and Jeff were charting this new territory, and I was about to join them.

One fall day, I had lunch with Dr. Duda, anxious to ask questions that had arisen during my studies. I walked into the little diner and saw Paul waiting for me. He felt like an old friend by now. I had been going once or twice a month to Adobe for several months, starting new groups and doing follow-up with the old ones.

Paul greeted me warmly and brought me up to date on "our boys." "Marilyn, you've been able to get more out of those boys with your presentation and that darn tape of yours in a few hours, than we get in months."

I replied, "Thanks for the good words, but I'm only the 'bottle opener.' If it weren't for you and your staff, I'd never attempt to do this type of therapy. You're the ones who do the really hard, consistent everyday work."

A wry smile crossed his tanned face as I continued, "But I need some help from you today. Some answers for my research. Not everyone who is abused becomes an offender. Do you see any consistency in the childhood abuse suffered by the boys you work with at Adobe?"

I pulled out a pad and pen as he began to talk. "I think there are three major contributing factors which cause a victim to turn into a violent offender. They relate to the offender's own childhood abuse: one, the amount of violence; two, the frequency of the abuse; and three, the closeness of the blood relationship between the offender and the victim."

Glancing up from my notes, I commented, "So, when a child, especially a boy, has those three things with intensity, the chances greatly increase for him to become a rapist or someone who is into anger and power."

"Precisely."

I gazed out the window at the fenced compound on the other side of the highway. I thought about each boy I had come to know in that place. "How about the child molestors? I've noticed that many of them have backgrounds of deprivation. They've never been loved or nurtured."

Paul reached for the check and said, "I think you're partially right. You know, my friends think I'm nuts to keep working out here. But those little shavers across the road have really gotten to me. They're all so needy and hurting and lonely. Sometimes I think I'm into burn-out, but I just can't walk away."

I could not walk away either. In fact I was no longer walking; I felt like my Feeling Adult was beginning to run.

I tucked myself away in my office and wrote on my legal pad as the thoughts flowed through. My new adult was taking advantage of all my inner resources. I bent over my note pad, oblivious to the time slipping past. I could not stop. I felt that somewhere there was a pattern to this abuse, a pattern as clear as a universal law. I put it all together to form what I called "The Law of Sustained Consequences":

A victim is a victim and, unless there is intervening therapy, the victim shall remain a victim, suffering the consequences of the wrongs inflicted upon him or her, with said consequences affecting not only this person but those within his or her sphere of influence, thus perpetuating it to future generations.

I received a call from Dr. Mazen the next day. "Marilyn, I've heard about your work at Adobe. When are you going to come down to the prison at Florence? We have about sixty men who could really benefit from your presentation. Think about it, please."

"I don't know, Sandy. Working with boys is one thing. Facing adult rapists and child molesters— that's something else. I'm not really sure I could do that."

My frontier was becoming wider each day, extending over mountains that looked as high and as awesome as the Himalayas.

Part Four

Developing the Feeling Adult

♦ 14 ♦

The Missing Piece

Adobe's prison gates swung open as I approached them, and as I walked through the prison, shouts of "Hi Marilyn!" echoed across the yard. I knew, if anyone ever tried to harm me, I would instantly be rescued by a group of very angry boys. After giving my presentation to six different groups of youthful offenders, I had a new, peculiar group of friends.

At Christmas, I spent several nights making dozens of cookies and homemade candies for a party at the prison. I bought each boy Leo Buscaglia's wonderful book, *Love*, and wrote a special message in the flyleaf of each book.

But I was not easy on those boys. I was there to help them understand what caused them to become offenders—not just to understand and recognize their own abusive backgrounds, but to be accountable for their present-day actions that resulted from their pasts.

Now that the boys felt comfortable with me, they no longer held back on their emotions or their language. I had heard every street word for sex there was, and if necessary, I probably could have sworn in three languages, languages which the boys referred to as "white, black, and Mexican."

Anger and pain often rocked the room.

"Man, I ain't to blame for raping that girl. It's my uncle's fault for raping *me*!" Jim's words spit from his mouth as he tossed his head in defiance.

"I know, Jim, I know. But while the people who abused you as a child were responsible for creating your Sobbing Hurting Child, you are still responsible for your own actions. Now you are also responsible for being the nurturing parent to that little hurting Jimmy inside your gut, for being the parent he so desperately needs."

I looked at these boys I had grown to love. How I wanted them to be free—free in every way. "The old way of doing things has locked you into a prison—not only this prison called 'Adobe,' but an emotional one, too. You don't have to stay locked up in either prison. You *can* change."

When the day was over, Paul and I had our usual glass of iced tea at the little diner across the road. My heart ached as he told me of overhearing some of the boys discussing what crime they needed to commit after their release in order to be re-sentenced to Adobe: not severe enough to end up in a maximum security prison, but back at Adobe. Adobe was their home, their life, everything they knew. For some, their group and Dr. Paul Duda were the only family they had.

These boys were scared. They were lonely. But they also wanted to belong, to be normal. They wanted to marry, to have families and jobs. But how? Who would hire a known child molester? Who would let their daughter marry a convicted rapist? What could they possibly look forward to? And none of them was yet eighteen years old.

Later the next day, during my session with Dr. Earle, I discussed some of my feelings regarding my work with the boys at Adobe.

Dr. Earle sat in his chair, his ankle resting on his knee, hands slightly touching his lips. When I finished, his hands dropped, his face expressing his pleasure. "I'm getting so excited about what you're doing that it's creating a dilemma for me. As your therapist, I want to caution you to slow down and take care of yourself. But as an interested professional, I want to encourage you in your work. Not a day goes by when I don't think of someone I want to meet you or to hear you speak."

Dr. Earle's contagious enthusiasm revived my sagging spirits over my situation at home.

I fluctuated daily, sometimes hourly, with feelings of hurt, excitement, frustration, exhilaration, loneliness, encouragement, anger, and empathy.

There were times my Sobbing Hurting Child still cried. I cried alone. I cried with Dr. Earle. I cried when I saw Dr. Danylchuk. I cried with Carol and Jeff.

I tried to ignore comments at home. It did not seem to matter anymore. There were so many other things to think about, things that kept me from looking at the separate paths Todd and I were taking.

The offers for speaking engagements and from therapists wanting to learn my theoretical concepts grew from a trickle to a steady stream.

I spent hours answering questions from a well-known psychologist. He became excited as he spoke. "I've studied many different theoretical concepts about personality structure. Each has its own terminology. Freud talks about the id, the ego, and the superego. Transactional analysis refers to the parent, adult, and child. Fairbairn uses specific terms in object relations like the central ego, the libidinal ego, and the anti-libidinal ego."

He looked at me and laughed aloud as he said, "But somehow 'anti-libidinal ego' just doesn't grab me in my gut like 'sobbing hurting child' does!"

In November, I took my presentation to Ottawa University in Kansas. As a result of an intensive publicity campaign, the auditorium was packed with students and professionals.

Standing at the podium, I felt as if I had come home. I looked out into the sea of friendly faces and noticed that many were young men. The little Marilyn peered out at the men, becoming frightened. *What if they don't like me! What if they think I'm ugly and dirty!* My adult reassured the little girl, and I proceeded with my talk.

It ended with a standing ovation and students lining up for counseling appointments. Four days later, I drove away, a piece of Ottawa still in my heart. The comments of the students and the president of the University gave me the courage I needed to face the next step of my homecoming.

Heading west, driving through rain that turned to sleet, I anticipated the warmth of returning home. My childhood town of Marion had not changed much, yet Main Street looked stark and uninviting. *It's lost something.* I looked at the river, the park, the stores. It used to be that returning home from a trip would mean feeling the whole town reach out to hug me, to welcome me home. Now it seemed a cold and distant stranger. The town no longer contained only happy memories: it had lost its innocence.

The bittersweet moment disappeared in the welcoming hugs and kisses of loving aunts, uncles, and cousins. The spread of food seemed better than I had remembered from my childhood. We laughed and caught up on each other's lives, yet only two relatives mentioned my therapy or the reason for it. All too soon, it was time to leave. Saying good-bye to elderly loved ones was difficult. I wondered if I would ever see some of them again.

I climbed in my rental car and again headed west, across the bridge and down the country road. The journey I was about to begin had started nearly three years before.

This day, my journey was taking me on a pilgrimage, to the place of my pain: *WICHITA*.

Wichita in November was cold and foreboding. The only spot of warmth came from my cousin John's house. I was curled up in an overstuffed chair, clothed in the warmth of velour sweats, a steaming mug of tea warming my hands.

"I don't think anything in my life happens by accident anymore," I commented.

John's thick eyebrows raised. "And what has not happened by accident now?"

"You. Your Ph.D. in psychology. Your work at the Veteran's Hospital. Who else would understand my search?"

Beth, John's wife, listened carefully. "Did you tell John about the letter to the advice columnist?"

"I forgot!" I turned to John, covering my tea with

my hand. "A woman who heard me speak called me to say she remembered reading a letter in a newspaper advice column. It was written by a man who had been a soldier in World War II and stationed in a Midwestern town."

John nodded, listening carefully.

"During that time, he was a participant in a gang rape in which a little girl was killed, but he was never arrested. He lived with the torment of that attack for the rest of his life."

I sipped my tea and then continued, "Do you think he might be one of my offenders?"

John thoughtfully considered the possibility. "We'll never know for sure, but perhaps . . ."

I could not sleep that night for all the ideas, questions, and memories tumbling in my head. I reviewed all I had done to prepare for this trip: phone calls to Wichita City Hall and obtaining a map of the city in 1944; talking to an old bus driver who remembered the bus routes driven during the war years.

Dawn came quickly, and I rose and dressed. I spread maps on the bed in front of me. I could feel the presence of a little girl beside me—my Sobbing Hurting Child. The child's hand trembled as she pointed to a street. "I remember that street. It's Hillside, where I used to live. I walked down that street to the store."

I quieted the little girl. "We need to find the church where choir practice took place, Little One. There are so many close by."

After numerous phone calls, I narrowed the possibilities to four. I felt like a detective looking for clues and following uncertain leads.

The Missing Piece

My exhilaration froze when the cold wind hit my face. The dark, overcast sky opened up to dump sleet onto the ground below. As I got in the car, I switched on the windshield wipers and waited for the heater to warm my chilled body. It took a few minutes to realize some of the shaking was not from the cold. In spite of my anxiety I began my journey down the familiar streets.

I sensed my Sobbing Child sitting on my lap, trembling from fear. "There it is," she said timidly, "Hillside Avenue. The big old house. Only it's not white anymore. Someone's painted it gray."

I parked across the street and gazed at the "bad house." I flipped through my stack of papers and maps to a manila envelope. Reaching inside, I removed a tattered photo. "Forty years ago, Little One. See? The tree is still the same. The porch railing is a little different. Do you think we should go inside?"

The only answer was a tremble.

"I think I'd like to sit in my bedroom and look at the big window that used to cause those awful nightmares."

The Sobbing Child gave little protest. My curiosity was stronger than my fear.

A "For Sale" sign had been staked into the front lawn. I crossed the street, walked up the stairs, and knocked on the door. No answer. I stood on the porch, memories spilling into my mind: memories of the boarders meeting boyfriends, while I sat on the steps, caring for my doll. Bigger, uglier memories tried to crowd in.

I knocked again and then left the porch. I wanted to peek into the windows, to see what I could, but I had to complete the journey: follow the bus routes into town, find the church, and then try to find the spot where the attack took place.

I drove to each church I had marked on my map—four churches that had been Evangelical United Bretheren, now Methodist. I knew immediately when I approached the right one. Its red brick exterior had not changed much.

From the church, I drove the first bus route toward home but nothing clicked. The homes were too nice, too established. I drove the next route, but again nothing: a missing puzzle piece searched for under the table and in the couch cushions.

I talked to the little girl, asking her questions: "Is this it, Little One?" "Where do we go from here?" The little girl was too confused to answer. I sighed, frustrated. I had followed each possible bus route from the church, then from home to the church. Nothing.

I drove from my school down another route. I looked from side to side, seeing nothing. Looking forward, I missed the turn to the church and traveled for several blocks. Suddenly, my breath caught in my throat. An invisible fist slugged my stomach.

Immediately in front of me, I could see the skyscrapers of downtown Wichita, looming as large as I had seen them once before—when I had put down my book after reading on the bus. I had missed my stop—the tall buildings were supposed to be far in the distance.

The memory of the sight burst over me.

The attack happened on the way to choir practice, not on my way home!

I struggled to hold the steering wheel of the car

as my wide-eyed child connected with the hurtling impact of recognition. *Dear God, this is the street! It happened here!*

The Sobbing Hurting Child was no longer in my lap. She *was* me. She snatched my breath away and shook my body. My eyes were seared by hot tears burning their way down my face. She ripped my gut as she tried to release a scream from deep within her terrified spirit.

She grabbed my body, making it stiffen as she began to twist my arms and legs. I fought to keep myself from surrendering to my nearly hysterical Sobbing Hurting Child, begging her to let me stay in control.

"Little One, listen to me! Nobody is going to hurt you now. The men aren't here anymore. Look around. See? The soldiers are gone. I'll protect you now. I'm finally strong enough."

"It's okay now, 's okay, 's okay, 's okay." I could hear the tiny voice chanting the words over and over as I hugged myself and rapidly patted my arms as if to keep my trembling body from disintegrating. The shaking gradually became only a slight tremor as I rocked back and forth while continuing to pat and soothe my Sobbing Child with "'s okay, 's okay." I lifted her into my arms and began to dry her eyes.

Minutes passed. I looked into the mirror to see my tear-streaked face. Despite the pain I saw there, I also saw the persistence and the will to survive. "All right, Little One, let's try to finish this up. We're almost done." My child stood beside me on the seat with her arms around my neck, burying her head in my shoulder as the car again started down the street.

As we drove, my Sobbing Hurting Child trembled again as she whispered, "Look, the trees have no leaves."

Fear sharpened my vision into the past. I could not help but see it—a gradual change, from established, solid, and clean to rundown, shabby, and poor. An invisible line, crossing from one skin color to the next, from one level of income to the next, from frustrations over what to have for dinner to fights over equality and prejudice.

I slowed the car and then stopped. We sat for a long moment, staring, hearts racing. Brick warehouses, eyes to the street and blind on the sides, extended to the back of long lots. Barren ground lay between them. Hedges. An occasional tree. Street lights impotent to cast light to the back of a lot.

I looked out of the car, my head moving from side to side, taking it all in. I stared at two of the buildings, wondering if they knew.

The buildings, old and silent, would not speak the secrets they knew. They would not tell of the screams they heard, of the violence they witnessed. The windowless walls had absorbed my screams and kept them from traveling out to the street.

As I drove by the vacant lots, flashes of memories lit up my mind. I saw the cars driving by, all the faces inside focused on the road ahead. They were not purposefully ignoring me; they could not hear—their windows rolled up against the cold, noisy heaters and radios filling the sound waves.

Whizzing past a dark, vacant lot, probably no one noticed a little girl. Perhaps they saw soldiers jousting in the snow, never imagining a terrified little girl was the brunt of their game.

I stopped the car. I felt as if I were wrestling with a struggling child as I stepped out onto the sidewalk. The little girl protested vehemently as I told her, "We have to do this. We have to prove we can walk down this street and not be hurt."

At five o'clock, the cloudy, dismal day had become even darker. I could barely see the hedges lining the sidewalk ahead. My teeth started to chatter, my body to shiver, tremble, and shake. Intense fear escalated until the Sobbing Hurting Child frantically began to claw and tear at my insides. "NO, NO, NO!!"

"Oh God, please, please help me get through this. It's okay, 's okay, Little One. Take my hand, we're going to make it."

Haltingly, my feet moving one step at a time, I approached the ominous hedges. Savage flashbacks streaked across my memory; I was certain that at any second incredible violence would burst upon me from behind that dreaded hiding place. The child was paralyzed with fear as tears filled her eyes until I could barely see the shrubs that were directly beside me.

Gradually, a shift began as my Feeling Adult emerged to encourage the terrorized child. "Little One, look up. Look around you. You are no longer eight years old. This is 1983, not 1944! Look, look behind the hedges. Those evil men aren't there anymore!"

Instead of being picked up and thrown into a

sadistic assault, I felt only silence. Brutal arms no longer came from nowhere to clamp and encircle my chest. Vicious hands no longer tore at my hair. Just silence. Quiet. A black couple with a darling little boy walked past and nodded hello as the boy looked up at me with a smile. As she returned his smile, my exhausted Sobbing Child reached out to take my hand. We walked back to the car.

I whispered to that brave child, "You've done a very special job today, Little One."

I thought of the people who questioned the validity of what happened. "How could you possibly *not* remember such an awful attack?" "If it had really happened, your mother would have known." "Was it oral rape? Was it anal rape? Just exactly how many men were there?" "How can you be certain you aren't just imagining all of it?"

My adult looked at the weary child snuggled beside me. "It doesn't matter! It doesn't matter what anyone else believes. I believe you. And I'm going to take care of you."

I knew I could not have imagined what I experienced this day. I was totally conscious as an adult, and the feelings were torrential.

The memories still were not sharp and clear—not like the photograph of that big, old white house. They probably never would be. They came in flashes: flashes of a street light reflected off shiny uniform buttons, flashes of naked tree limbs stretched out over a small child.

Then today, the largest flash of all: the sight of the skyscrapers bursting over me, like a shower of fireworks on a Kansas Fourth of July.

Today, the feelings and the memories matched.

The Missing Piece

Peace was slowly beginning to surround my past. "Little One, we can go home now. All the pieces to the puzzle are in place at last."

But were they?

♦ 15 ♦

Sand and Fire

Codependency—the psychological buzzword of the late eighties and ninties.

There are many definitions of a codependent. Briefly it applies to any person who sacrifices her or his self-worth by submitting to, and taking responsibility for, another person, thus enabling the other person to engage in destructive behavior. A codependent person is usually a product of a restrictive culture or society that teaches that strong personal boundaries are selfish and wrong.

In the early eighties I knew nothing about codependency. I had heard the word *enabler* (the same as a *codependent*), but I thought it applied only to spouses of alcoholics or addicts. It couldn't possibly apply to me. Todd was nearly a teetotaler.

I was a classic codependent. My culture, my heritage, and my church taught me to be a codependent. I was taught that it was, in fact, the optimum for a woman: to be a self-sacrificing and submissive caretaker. Work hard, be perfect, do not have needs, be responsible, do not be prideful. Then I came home from therapy and demanded that after twenty-five years, all of us should change. I became angry, hurt, and frustrated when that did not happen. Of course it could not happen—not while we lived in our old boundaries—because that same culture, heritage, and church told us we should not change.

In 1989, I read books on codependency that would have been lifesavers for me in 1981. I could have handed them to Todd, to my family, to my church friends, and said, "Here, read this. This is me. Yes, I'm a victim of sexual abuse. But that's not the only reason I am sick, emotionally and physically. If my attack had never happened, I'd still be sick. Sick from years and years of unresolved conflict, of pushing down my own needs, of trying to save the whole world and feeling guilty for not saving it fast enough." But I did not have those books for them or for me.

Fortunately, I began to listen to Dr. Danylchuk and to Dr. Earle. My Feeling Adult knew they were correct when they said that I had to take care of myself, that no one else was responsible for me but me. But accepting that was difficult and not always possible. My Controlling Child often succumbed to my old tapes of responsibility and self-sacrifice, messages that were daily reinforced by the tapes of the codependent world in which I lived.

I had anticipated 1984 would be a hard year. But if I had known how hard, I might have stopped it before it began.

At the start of the year, I noticed an increase in my lifelong sensitivity to light. The first indication came during a routine appointment with the optometrist. As he examined my eyes, I felt driven through the back of the chair with the light. A few days later, as I typed, a tiny light on the face of the typewriter moved slowly across the machine. As it did, I could not move my eyes away. The light nearly hypnotized me.

As the light stopped, I fell deeper and deeper into the black pit I thought I had left in Burlingame. The slimy tentacles of the cold walls reached out to grab me and torment me with light. Then, it was a man holding a light, coming closer, closer to my eyes, ignoring my screams for mercy. I wanted to close my eyes, but something, someone, forced me to keep them open.

When the flashback ended, I wondered where it had come from. After so many hours in therapy, each moment of the attack scrutinized many times, I could not imagine that anything else could have happened. I hoped whatever it was would stay buried—forever, if possible.

Life with Todd continued to deteriorate; it was clear that what I wanted and needed was a *growing* relationship. With the stress, my pain level escalated again to a "suicidal ten." The impact on my body forced me to confront the decision I did not want to make: a decision to end the marriage. In a letter to a friend I wrote:

> I don't know how long I would continue to stay if I felt well physically. I keep thinking of our two mutual friends who died of cancer in their 40's. I really feel that repressed emotional pain destroys the immune system. I don't want to be a martyr at 47!
>
> I'm also finally realizing that emotional pain is surely just as destructive as physical pain. I will not survive in a relationship that is not a

mutually supportive and a mutually nurturing one, nor one in which I am not acknowledged as an individual person or accepted for who and what I am.

Even without the physical pain, of one thing I am certain, if I had stayed, it would have meant reimprisoning my Original Child, a child now filled with wonderment, creativity, and emerging self-worth. It would have meant taking this joyous child and walking her back into her old cell of solitary confinement, there to remain for the rest of her life.

Todd? Or the child?

After we had a final session with Dr. Earle I realized that we had reached an unresolvable impasse. I had done everything I knew to do. Other major conflicts occurred that signaled the end. My intense frustration and anger began to dissolve into deep regret and sorrow. Nothing seemed to change our situation. I had run out of options.

For the last time I looked at the interior of the house I loved. I had drawn the plans and supervised the contractors. I had decorated it with love and pride. With blurred eyes, I glanced at the calendar as I walked out the door: April 1, 1984—our twenty-eighth wedding anniversary. How ironic.

Steeling myself, I climbed into my overloaded car and drove past the palms and out of the curving drive forever. The desert around me was bleak. *Could this road leading me west to California be wrong for me?* Waves of guilt, confusion, and pain blew over me like the dust billowing in the sand dunes outside my car windows.

The invisible waves penetrated the windows.

The emotional sand burned my eyes. Blinded by the pain, I pulled off to the side of the road. My head rested on the steering wheel as my sobs rolled through. They ripped through my chest and throat. They tore my heart apart. The word *divorce* raged through me, shrieking with pain. I wondered if I could walk through this and make it to the other side.

Dear God. How did we ever come to this? How I hate this. I never knew it would hurt so much.

♦ ♦ ♦

San Mateo, ten miles south of San Francisco, opened its arms to accept me. I walked into an empty condominium and smiled. Babette followed me, looking around at the huge windows, the small balcony, and the towering redwood tree. "It looks like you could be very happy here. You certainly deserve it."

The condominium soon reflected the new Marilyn. Instead of the heavy masculine influence of dark paneled walls and massive furniture of my home in Scottsdale, the condominium took on life with white carpeting and furniture in shades of mauve with lavender accents. My Original Child enjoyed herself immensely.

A short time later, I prepared to return to Scottsdale for a radical hysterectomy. I braced myself for the anticipated difficult time talking to people from church. I felt that as friends came to visit me after the surgery, they would probably question the wisdom of my drastic decision. I counseled with Dr. Danylchuk, and he helped me prepare some appropriate answers to the negative comments I expected regarding my divorce.

A month after my surgery, I returned to California, grappling with feelings of hurt, rejection, and anger. The one thing I had not prepared for was the fact that, except for one couple, no one from my church (other than family and MORE THAN FRIENDS women) came to visit during the entire three weeks. I was not neglected during that time. I received flowers, calls, cards, and visits from others. But to most of the people from church, it seemed I did not exist.

Back in my new home in San Mateo, all my reading about divorce and its difficult adjustments did not fully prepare me for the stunning realities—not only of rejection by friends, but of the simple "aloneness" of it all. After twenty-eight years of marriage, it was hard to go to bed alone and wake up alone. It was not that I had never gone to bed alone—there were Todd's many hunting trips. It was knowing that the empty space beside me would not be filled, not in a few days, possibly never.

Dinner alone. Never walking into a room where someone else made a mess. No one to talk to at night. It was large. Frightening. Lonely.

I had very little energy to progress with my life. I was not recuperating well from my surgery, and the familiar headaches were escalating with startling intensity. My local gynecologist attempted to adjust my hormone treatment in the hope of reducing my pain level. Despite repeated changes in prescriptions, not only did the headaches worsen, but my temperature began to rise. I shopped for vitamin supplements and sleeping pills, trying to find some peace from all the pain.

My skin erupted in an alarming rash of hives, screaming its reaction to the drugs. A dermatologist ordered daily injections and no more pain medication until the rash cleared.

Tears came to my eyes. "You don't understand. The pain is so bad, it's pushing old buttons for me. I'm beginning to feel suicidal again. I need the medication to keep the pain below the level I cannot tolerate."

Dr. Danylchuk suggested I try daily therapeutic massage, thinking it could keep the edge off my pain while I allowed my body to cleanse itself from the drugs. Thankfully, it worked, keeping my pain just below the self-destruct threshold.

Two weeks later, the doctor was still puzzled. "I'm concerned because your temperature is still registering 102, and I've no idea what's causing it."

"I keep having chills. My fever seems to top out at 103 every day about four o'clock. It hasn't dropped below 100 in over a week."

The doctor's hands disappeared into white pockets. "The blood tests done yesterday are all negative. I don't know what else medically we can do for you."

He leaned against the wall, and continued. "Because a hysterectomy is a 'sexual' surgery, I'm aware that it can sometimes activate memories if the patient has a history of sexual abuse. I'm wondering if that's what happened to you. Have you considered returning to therapy with Dr. Danylchuk?"

I was amazed. "I talked to my gynecologist in

Scottsdale this morning, and he told me exactly the same thing."

At home, I waited for Dr. Danylchuk to call. He had gone on a camping vacation, promising to call during the week to see how I was feeling. "Marilyn," he said, "I've been thinking about another client. She had a hysterectomy, and it stirred up a lot of old memories of sexual abuse. Do you think that could possibly be at the root of your intense headaches now?"

I sat heavily on my bed. "Pete, this can't be a coincidence. You're the third person who has suggested that correlation. What are the chances of my doing some therapy with you before I leave for Arizona in two weeks?"

"Even if I have to work nights and weekends, I'll work you in. Don't worry. We'll get you well. You and I haven't struggled through all this hell making you a whole person to let you disintegrate now!"

His familiar therapy room welcomed me back. Violent words again gushed from some ugly pit deep inside me. But these words were new, different words.

My Sobbing Hurting Child was terrorized. "Don't take me down there! It's bad. I don't want to go down there. It's scary. Please don't take me down in that hole!

"I don't want to do this anymore. I'm so tired. Please don't hurt my head anymore. I don't want to see the light. Don't know what the light is. No! No! Take it away! Fire. Fire. Face is so hot. Please, please don't hurt me anymore."

Violent hysteria plunged me into the depths of

my pit. I was falling faster and deeper than I had ever gone before.

"Take the light away. Take it away. Take it away! Oh please, no, no, no, NOT MY EYES! NOT MY EYES! Oh dear God please! TAKE THE LIGHT AWAY!

"Please, Pete help me stop. It's never been this bad! I cannot stand this!"

As Dr. Danylchuk soothed my Sobbing Child, his voice sounded troubled. "I've sat here for hundreds of hours with you as you've relived that rape. But I'm certain you felt the most intense panic and terror today that I've ever seen you experience. What's the light? What in the world are they doing to you?"

Shaking and sobbing, I stammered, "I don't know. I don't know. Except whatever it is—it's, it's so terrifying it's causing me to feel like I'm going insane. Actually going 'over the line' into insanity."

The days passed, ugly days with new knowledge, terrifying and hideous: being held upside down and carried into a black hole—maybe a storm cellar. The circle of men, only the whites of their eyes and white teeth showing, laughing, coming closer, closer, closer, with a cigarette lighter. Forcing me to keep my eyes open.

Telling me they were going to burn out my eyes.

My Sobbing Child knew they would follow through with their sadistic promise. Hadn't they already fulfilled all their other threats?

Terror beyond belief combined with one final burst of my will to survive. New strength surged from a nearly destroyed inner core. In the ensuing frenzy, I was knocked unconscious.

Left for dead. Waking, now feeling insane. The little child writhed, white and naked on the black dirty ground. Small hands clawed the air, bizarre sounds spilled from my throat. Animal sounds. Snarling. Vicious. Insane.

I watched from a distance, my heart breaking. I approached the tormented little child, scooped her up into my arms. "Poor, poor baby. I can't leave you like this. I won't leave you like this. I promise you, I'll take care of you."

That night I picked up my old journal and began to write of feelings that were no longer just my feelings but those of children throughout the world.

Screams, echoing the sounds of madness,
sear their imprint into time and space.
In centuries containing myriads of
   terrorized children,
as little ones are pulled over the edge,
into a pit holding inexplicable horror.
Insanity twists its bony fingers into the soft,
pliable mass of an innocent mind,
sadistically reveling in the torment,
as clawlike hands rip away the fragile shreds
   of reality.

Later, Dr. Danylchuk and I, two rational, intelligent adults, sat in a room, discussing the insane child.

I shook my head, still in agonizing wonder over the new information uncovered. "In my theory, I say that some children, as a result of severe trauma, can go over a line into psychosis. Now I'm certain I'm correct. When I wrote that, I didn't realize I had personally experienced that myself."

With eyebrows raised, Dr. Danylchuk commented, "Well, your unconscious certainly did. Fortunately you had a strong innate personality and loving, nurturing parents. As a result, your ego strength was better than average for an eight-year-old."

I propped myself up on my familiar pillow and continued his thought. "Consequently, I was able to split and form a strong Controlling Child. She totally buried my insane child in order for the essence of Marilyn Reh to survive."

Dr. Danylchuk rocked back in his low chair beside me. "Think of how many people are not as fortunate as you. They end up in mental institutions."

"Pete, I firmly believe that the ability to split when pain becomes severe is what keeps a child sane."

As we continued to talk and theorize, I remembered the hours in this room when my adult had struggled between sanity and insanity, between life and death.

I looked at Dr. Danylchuk's strong, gentle hands resting on his knees. Holding on to those hands had been my only lifeline for so long. My child and my adult had both desperately needed him, his wisdom and his strength, to survive. Yes, I had become dependent on him (and Babette) while I was in therapy. A terrorized eight-year-old is dependent as hell.

Dr. Danylchuk was the one who helped me find and nurture my Original Feeling Child. As a therapist, mentor, and friend, I loved him dearly. He had saved my life.

But that was nearly four years ago. Since then, I had consciously worked on expanding my support system. Because of my terrorizing "light," I again found myself needing Dr. Danylchuk for this ten days of therapy. But other than that, my dependency on him had faded until it was almost nonexistent. It felt like a sign of health.

♦ 16 ♦

Fragile Armor

Two days later, I surveyed the woman in the bath-room mirror, her eyes no longer bleeding with pain: from Burlingame to Phoenix, from excruciating pain to healing, from therapy room to speakers' convention.

I applied my lipstick, remembering Florence Littauer's advice to speakers, "Always look profes-sional and always be prepared to tell your story in just three minutes."

Three minutes! How in the world could I possi-bly condense my own story to only three minutes!

I dabbed my lips, straightened my skirt, and tried to keep my fear at bay. Not only was I preparing to attend my first National Speakers Association con-vention, but there was the remote chance I would be asked to speak that morning. Each newcomer was asked to place his or her business card in a hat. Two, out of the several hundred first-timers, would be chosen to give an extemporaneous three-minute speech.

I sat down next to my sister, Mary Sue, and six other members of the CLASS staff, just as the an-nouncer took a card from the hat and said, "Our first speaker this morning will be Marilyn Murray."

Mary Sue gasped, but I was not really surprised. As I walked to the podium, I kept remembering: there are no accidents.

In less than two minutes, after my final words, the crowd burst into a standing ovation. Afterwards, a tall man approached me. "Hello, my name is Richard. I wonder if we could meet during lunch tomorrow. I'd really like to know more about what you're doing."

Our luncheon conversation was so animated that we resumed at dinner and stayed past midnight. As we prepared to say goodnight, I showed Richard my photos and handwriting samples from my time in therapy.

"Marilyn," he said, amazed, "that can't possibly be you! I never would have recognized you."

As his eyes scanned the lined journal sheet on which I had scrawled, "I can't write, I'm only eight," he pointed to a sentence midway on the page. "Look, you wrote, 'The light hurts my eye.' You told me you had no memory of the 'light' until recently. Yet you wrote this immediately after your 'volcano' nearly four years ago. See, your unconscious was trying to tell you about that torturing light from the very beginning."

I stared at the page. "I'd never noticed that before. I remember that, right after I wrote it, I thought the sentence referred to the *car lights* that haunted me so much."

The next morning in the breakfast buffet line, I noticed Richard approaching, looking drawn and somewhat disheveled, very unlike his former elegant appearance.

"Lady, your one-minute-and-fifty-five-second talk yesterday changed my life. Last night, after I left you, I went for a very long walk. My dad died last year, and I've never let myself grieve for him. Talking with you gave me permission to get in touch with my feelings and start to face my own hurt."

His voice broke as he continued, "I spent the entire night on the desert, allowing myself to cry for my dad for the very first time. What an incredibly healing experience!"

For three days, people stopped me in the halls, in the restrooms, in quiet corners: all sharing the pain of their childhood. They hugged me; they thanked me.

That night at the closing banquet, my mind tumbled. *Lord, all this can't have "just happened." You keep skimming me through this so fast, I can't keep up. How do you think these people would react if they knew what I'm going to be doing tomorrow?*

Back in my room, I hung up my sequined gown. I glanced at the clock, realizing I would have only a few hours of sleep.

Dawn came too quickly. I rose and put on a plain denim skirt and oxford cloth blouse. I put my jewelry in my suitcase and checked the mirror to be certain my makeup and hair looked as inconspicuous as possible. I slipped out of the hotel, away from a world of glamor and excitement, a world where freedom and security are taken for granted, and prepared to step into a totally different realm, where such luxuries do not exist.

That morning, in southern Arizona, adult rapists and child molesters waited for me to give my first presentation within a maximum security prison.

"Look over there, Marilyn. There it is."

My eyes followed Dr. Mazen's outstretched hand as his car sped along the empty desert road. The prison, still far away, looked small and insignificant.

"Marilyn, I can't tell you how pleased I am that you've finally decided to come. I know it wasn't an easy decision for you. I've been telling the men about you for three years. We already have a long list of men waiting to hear you speak."

"I wonder how many of them will still want to come after they hear about my infamous tape from today's participants."

Dr. Mazen maintained his enthusiasm. "I think you'll be surprised by their courage. The Sex Offender Treatment Program is located in two trailers at the far end of the trustee yard. Sometimes it takes several years for a man to have the guts to 'walk the gauntlet' across that long open space to those trailers."

"I can't imagine how difficult it must be. Everyone would then know they are sex offenders."

"Right. In prison, a sex offender is on the very bottom of the 'pecking order' and is often considered fair game for severe abuse by the other inmates. When he takes that first scary trip toward the trailers, he is identifying himself as a rapist or child molester. Consequently, an offender must have a genuine desire to change before he makes the trip."

"So this isn't just to get a good-behavior certificate in their prison file?"

"Oh no. In fact, I've found most of the men in our program here work a lot harder in therapy than the majority of my clients on the outside."

"How many of the men imprisoned in Florence are sex offenders?"

Dr. Mazen looked somewhat amused. "That's the irony of it all. I think probably the majority of the inmates in this prison have a sex offense of some kind in their background. Most have never been convicted of it or have plea-bargained to a different offense just so they won't have it on their record."

Conversation between us faded as Dr. Mazen turned off the main road. Our destination now loomed large and formidable directly in front of us: Arizona State Prison Florence—an expanse of concrete spread over the dusty ground, surrounded by high fences edged in razor wire.

Armed guards on horseback patrolled the fields outside the walls, and prisoners weeded long rows of cotton. The early morning sun shimmered in the water from the irrigation ditches that brought moisture to the dry, parched desert. The bright green plants sprang from the ground, seeming incongruous next to the tall watchtowers with their gun turrets and uniformed sentries.

The guard at the gate checked Dr. Mazen's badge. We waited as he searched for my name on the clipboard in his hand, then finally waved us through.

Dr. Mazen parked the car. I took a deep breath as I started my own long dusty walk toward those innocuous looking trailers.

The July morning had already passed 100 degrees. I welcomed the rush of cool air as I stepped inside. The men I saw there looked like any ordinary group of friends standing around visiting; but these men were serving sentences ranging from five years to life. *What goes on inside those heavily armored exteriors? What if I can't disarm those shields? What if I fail?*

As the men began to take their seats, I mentally went through the list Dr. Mazen had given me:

- George: Caucasian, age 29, convicted of rape and assault, sentenced to thirty years in prison, served six years.
- Tony: Hispanic, age 26, convicted of rape, sentenced to seven to seventeen years in prison, served five years.
- Carl: Black, age 29, convicted of rape, sentenced to ten to twenty years in prison, served seven years.
- Tom: Caucasian, age 38, convicted of child molestation, sentenced to five years in prison, served three years.
- David: Caucasian, age 38, convicted of child molestation, sentenced to five years in prison, served three years.
- Earl: Black, age 35, convicted of rape, sentenced to thirty years in prison, served ten years.
- Harry: Caucasian, age 63, convicted of child molestation, sentenced to five years in prison, served three years.
- Joey: Hispanic/caucasian, age 32, convicted of rape, sentenced to forty years to life in prison, served thirteen years.

I swallowed. *Are you sure this is what you want me to do, Lord? This isn't going to be easy!*

Praying silently, I stood at the front of the room and began: "No, no, not me! I had a perfect childhood."

The men seemed more attentive than I expected—that is, all but one. George placed his chair several feet outside the semicircle. His body language shrieked messages of "Stay away!" as he slid down into his seat, his arms firmly crossed over his chest. He pulled his hat so far down over his face, I could not see his eyes.

Relaxing in the chair nearest me sat Earl, looking at me with a cocky grin, a grin that enveloped his whole being as he exuded the vision of "Joe Cool." His defense mechanism, while more socially acceptable than George's, was still effective.

Carl, strong and hardened, proudly wore his large Afro. He surprised me with his tears as I described my volcano. They glistened on his dark face as he made no move to hide their presence.

"That house, that bad house, soldiers, wartime, the bombs are falling!"

A jacket emblazoned with a multicolored dragon and the word "Saigon" rustled in the corner as its wearer smashed his fourth cigarette into the coffee-can ashtray. Tom pulled at his scraggly beard as he tried to dissociate himself from memories of the crashing of artillery and the screams of terrified children and wounded buddies.

"Dear God, please don't let this happen to me!"

David choked on his tears as he fingered the little cross pinned on his collar. *I wonder if he's someone who uses his Christianity as a defense, feeling he doesn't need to work on his problems because now they've all been forgiven!*

"... and I remained an eight-year-old for six weeks. Here's a sample of my handwriting."

Grandfatherly looking Harry leaned forward in his chair, nodding with interest as each new slide appeared on the screen. He smiled gently at me as I turned the lights back on and reached for my bottles representing "pools of pain."

"This bottle represents a boy whose father and mother show him no love at all."

The past surprised Joey with its pain. The overwhelming emotions hit him so suddenly, uncontrolled tears poured out. He gripped the chair, struggling to regain control as I continued speaking.

Tony, uncomfortable with his friend's deep emotions, kept his eyes riveted to the floor. Years of conditioning had constructed a nearly impenetrable barrier. A macho man never cried, especially a Chicano.

"Sometimes it takes a very long time to empty out this pool."

Nearly two hours had passed as I prepared to close my part of the presentation. "I realize in this prison, you are regarded as the 'lowest of the low.' How many times have you felt that 'nobody gives a damn' about you, that nobody cares? Well, I want you to know, *I care*. If I didn't care, I wouldn't be here. I don't get paid for this, and I pay all my own expenses to fly here. You see, I'm here because I believe you are men of worth and value, persons who have a right to be given the opportunity to change.

"But that change will be one of the most difficult things you've ever done. You have to accept full responsibility for the offenses that placed you here. You also must be willing to look deep inside your gut and take out that hurting little boy that's in there. You have to allow little Joey or Davey or Tommy to tell you what happened to him to make him lash out with so much hurt and anger toward other people.

"One of the reasons I'm here today is to help you with that process." I pulled the tape recorder to me as I began to explain to the men what they were about to see and hear.

Their bodies tensed in anticipation as I picked up the tape. "Look at my face and remember it well as you listen to what sexual abuse can do to a child, to a woman. Never forget the sound of that pain."

Despite my many sessions at Adobe, I still felt unprepared for the impact of seeing my child's innocent smile fill the screen while bathed in the violent torment of her screams.

I forced myself to look at each man: muscular arms folded and unfolded, sweaty hands clasped and unclasped, nervous legs crossed and uncrossed. Rough knuckles became white as they clung to the edge of the chairs. Frantic eyes darted about the room looking for an escape from the child's relentless agony. Gradually, the extreme tension eased, to be replaced by a wave of deep personal sorrow. It was as though each offender first felt his victim's pain and then slowly began to touch his own.

As the lights went back on, nearly every face was bathed in tears. George headed for the door and left without a word.

Carl haltingly began to tell a story of long-term sexual abuse. "She wouldn't believe me. I told my mom what those older girls were doing to me, and she wouldn't believe me. She whipped me for lying!"

I tried to hide my surprise. I had been told that Carl rarely shared in any group, much less revealed abuse.

"Man, I come from a rough neighborhood," he continued. "There was nobody to protect the kids. You had to learn how to be tough to survive. The boys thought it was cool that I got to have sex so young. But I hated it. It felt real bad. I felt so alone. I thought my mom and my sisters hated me. I thought I was the one who was always wrong and bad. Then I finally decided I'd just go ahead and be bad. I ain't got nothing to lose. But I did lose. I ended up in here. I wouldn't listen to anyone, didn't care about anyone's feelings. I was ignorant of what life is really all about."

Joey turned to Carl. "Yeah, I know what that's like. I was molested by my aunt when I was only four. I always felt I was bad, I was the guilty one."

Dr. Mazen had told me about Joey and his potential. Joey was soon to take over as administrative assistant for the SOTP program and would be responsible for all the scheduling and coordinating of the sessions. He had taken almost all the college courses offered in the prison program, becoming knowledgeable in psychology, sociology, philosophy, and more. He was highly articulate (he read the dictionary daily), good looking, and a part of a special team of inmates that previously spoke in Arizona schools to warn of the dangers of drug and alcohol abuse. His presence and words impressed teenagers with the hard realities of prison life. Yet in prison, potential did not matter. Unless granted parole, Joey would not be released until the year 2012.

Tom spoke in response to Joey, "Yeah, I know how it feels to be so hurt. The army trained me to be a killer; that's what I do best. God, I'd like to do that to my old man! Tried to once, when I was twelve. He took me into the desert and beat me with a club and a whip. Then he left me out there, all alone, for four days. Then he beat up my mom, broke my jaw, and I ended up with over a hundred stitches in my head. Right after that I decided I'd kill him. Unfortunately, all I had was a .22 and I only wounded him. When I found out he wasn't dead, I ran away. I guess I've been running ever since."

Earl spoke up, "Man, I didn't have a childhood nothing like you guys. My parents were good to me. I can't really relate to anything you say." He glanced at me and smiled, heading toward the door. "Sorry, but I gotta go now."

Tony acted as though he wanted to follow Earl, but he looked at Joey and decided to stay. "I can't talk about what happened to me when I was a kid. In my family, it's an unwritten law that you *never, ever* talk to anyone else about anything that's wrong in the family, especially if you're a man. A man always stays strong and quiet, no matter what."

Joey sensed Tony's distress and encouraged him. "It's okay, it's safe here. Nobody here's going to tell your family. It's really important that you finally let go of some of the deep hurt that I know you're carrying around."

Tony's broad shoulders trembled as he shook his head, "No, no."

I reached out and touched his clenched fist. "Oh, Tony, I know a little bit how you feel. When I found out about my attack, some of my family didn't want me to talk about it either. It was the most difficult decision I ever made in my life—to decide to do what was best for me in order to stay alive, even though I knew it would hurt the family I loved. That's such a painful choice to have to make. Please take care of Tony. Only you can do that."

Tony silently struggled with my words as Joey put an arm around his friend's shoulder. Gradually the group continued sharing their feelings and reactions to the day's events.

David spoke up, "When I looked at your bottles I could really see my own 'pool of pain.' My parents beat me with a pitchfork. But I've learned how to forgive them since I've become a Christian. I know what's past is past, and I have to release all my hate to the Lord. 'Old things are passed away, behold all things have become new.' My sins have been buried in the 'sea of forgetfulness.' I know I'll never offend again as long as I keep my Bible right here beside me."

Several pairs of eyes rolled heavenward, reflecting the general attitude of the rest of the group. While many of the new Christians gained respect due to their manner of living which reflected genuine life-changes, others who had become "Bible-thumpers" were seen as using God's forgiveness as an excuse for refraining from honestly dealing with their own offenses.

An hour after he had left, Earl returned, pain strangling his voice. "You're right, man. I *was* abused."

The men continued pouring out their childhood pain. As they did, they struggled even more with the pain they had caused their victims. Some wanted to deny it, but the other men would not let the denial remain. They pushed, they encouraged, they struggled to deal with the ugliness of it all.

After seven hours, I stood at the door saying good-bye. I gave every man a hug. Each waited his turn—hesitant, respectful, unbelieving.

How long has it been since some of them have felt a woman's touch? Certainly not one from a rape victim. They fought back their tears, not too successfully. I joined them.

That day I saw not rapists and child molesters, but deeply hurting human beings. I saw human beings who were created with an Original Feeling Child, a child that had been battered and beaten into nonexistence. Now, all that was left was a tough, lonely little boy standing in the middle of a prison yard, trying to stay alive.

Looking over my shoulder as we drove out the gate, I saw those hurting children: little boys in grown up bodies, watching through the razor-wire fence as Dr. Mazen and I drove out to freedom.

My life changed at that moment. My frontier no longer only reached forward. Now it also reached backward, pulling me back to Arizona, back to prison—a prison where I found pain, but also healing.

♦ 17 ♦

Rhumbas and Rockets

The music pulsed and flowed, shifting the air in the room. I moved with my partner, feeling awkward and free at the same time. John led me through a smooth fox trot, then a fun swing, and a heated cha-cha.

Dancing. Before therapy, my legs hurt too much to think about dancing. Now, my Original Feeling Child wanted to dance. So I treated her to dancing lessons, to dance and exercise at the same time and the opportunity to meet some new friends: old needs never acknowledged, now being met in one simple act.

Dancing exceeded my expectations for fun, exercise, and friendship. It became my therapy. I had always been so rigid. Learning to feel good about moving my body to the music was a major stepping stone for me.

My instructor, John, became a close friend. His Original Feeling Child and mine had a wonderful time. He taught me to play; I taught him to explore his inner self. I shared my knowledge of art; he shared his knowledge of the theater. We explored the endless corners of San Francisco from restaurants to discos, from the punk community to the gay community.

One evening, at a table overlooking Fisherman's Wharf, John made an offhand statement that hurt my feelings. Years of prior conditioning overrode hours of therapy. Without being aware of it, I immediately withdrew.

After a few seconds of silence, John's impish eyes swept the ceiling as he declared, "Oops, I think I just heard the lid on your box close!"

Slowly, deliberately, I pushed open the lid of my old box. Taking myself by the nape of the neck, I pulled out my protesting Sobbing Hurting Child and made her sit on top of the table and look John in the face. My Controlling Child, no longer sitting on top of the box, decided it was safe to step aside. She allowed us to sit for hours talking about our feelings.

It was the first time I had a personal conflict, outside of therapy, in which knowing about the three "children" provided a language to resolve a problem. The reconciliation was accomplished with words that were not threatening or hostile, and even contained some humor.

Learning how to use my theoretical concepts in my personal relationships was one thing, but now I was anxious to learn more about their usefulness therapeutically.

For several months, Dr. Danylchuk and his wife, Lynette, had been discussing the possibility of opening their own counseling center in San Mateo, a center that specialized in regressive therapy. Restoration Therapy Center became a reality in October 1984, and I went to work there as an intern.

Dr. Danylchuk's long list of clients, combined with many referrals as a result of my continuing presentations around the country, kept the center filled.

I had more than a thousand hours of personal therapy, had counseled hundreds as a result of my talks, and had worked at the CASA for nearly a year and part-time at the prisons for several years. But I still had a lot to learn.

One of the center's first clients came as a result of one of my presentations at a CLASS seminar. The morning she arrived, I walked into my therapy room to find her huddled in the corner—a small cowering form, looking much like a fragile twelve-year-old, even though she was a twenty-eight-year-old mother of three.

"Hello little one, may I sit here beside you?"

The head moved up and down, almost imperceptibly.

As the hours passed, I became intimately acquainted with Cathy's five different personalities, one of whom was a two-year-old who had never spoken to anyone before. Cradling the newly emerged "Misty" in my arms, I slowly convinced her to take my hand and go with me into an imaginary secret garden where she could play with tiny animals and always be safe.

As I rocked the small child, I thought of her molestation by her father and brother. Both men were active in their church and vehemently denied the accusation.

As the days passed, new information came forth, disturbing information. Cathy had been in five mental hospitals, diagnosed as manic depressive and schizophrenic. Only recently had someone discovered her multiple personalities. At the hospitals, as she regressed, instead of being allowed to release the painful memories, she had been heavily sedated, tied and/or strapped down, and then sent to a lock-up ward with a burly guard standing over her. One guard had even put a pillow over her head every time she cried or screamed.

Each therapy session at our center revealed more of each personality: Cathy, the functioning adult; Misty, the two-year-old; Tammy, the hostile, self-destructive, angry one; Marcia, the mother, protector, and caretaker; and Penny, the five-year-old chatterbox.

The small children within Cathy reminded me of myself during my time in therapy. Cathy asked for crayons and a coloring book. I gladly gave her the ones I used during my time in therapy. She clutched them tightly in her lap, not understanding the significance of the gift.

Remembering the lonely weekends I spent in Burlingame while "eight," I drove to Babette's to pick up Cathy and spend Saturday with her. The hours of the day flowed together with personalities, tears, laughter, and wonder at seeing the world through eyes that had been blinded with pain.

As darkness pushed away the light, I drove a tired bundle home to Babette's. I walked with Cathy into the familiar bedroom with the flowered wallpaper pattern memorized by my terrified eight-year-old.

I tucked her into the bed, gently laying her doll next to her. Leaning over, I kissed them both. "Good night, little one. I love you. I am here."

As I slipped out the door, I paused to take one last look. *Lord, I never knew, during all those painful nights, that one day I'd come full circle and be standing here with someone else lying in my place.*

Day after day, I sat on the mat, absorbed with Cathy's therapy. Instinctively, I seemed to know what was going to happen next within the jumbled labyrinth of Cathy's emotions. At the end of the final day's session, Cathy looked at me in wonder. "I don't understand. No matter what corner of my mind I try to escape to, when I get there, you're already sitting there waiting for me. You reach deep inside me and gently lift out each part of me and help us to feel. No one has ever been able to reach those hidden children in me that you've been able to touch."

She threw her arms around me in a hug. "For the first time, I'm beginning to realize I'm not crazy! When you explained your theory to me last week, all the parts of me could comprehend it, even Misty. It made us all feel so good to know somebody at last understands about people like us and doesn't think we're weird or strange or ought to be locked up."

As we said our good-byes, I knew Dr. Danylchuk, Lynette, and I had played a small part in Cathy's journey toward wholeness. I wanted to be a part of that healing journey for many others.

I also knew that my own journey was not over yet, that it would never be completely over. It now had placed me on the front lines—counseling clients at the center, giving my personal presentation throughout the country, working with Dr. Danylchuk on conferences and workshops, traveling to the prison in Arizona several times a year, and studying in a doctoral program.

Dancing helped drain the stress. After concentrating on a rhumba or tango, the day's problems with clients remained on the shelf, and I could go home and sleep. One day, John suggested that I perform in a ballroom dance competition. I rejected the idea at first, but my Original Feeling Child begged me to reconsider, and I gave in. Endless practice hours followed, some hours outrageously fun, and all of them great exercise.

In Acapulco, at an international contest, I glanced at the mirrored walls of the ballroom as John whirled me around the floor. I saw the reflection of a slim, tanned blonde floating on a cloud of white feathers, swirling in a magical myriad of sparkling crystals. As she twirled and spun, suddenly I was startled to realize, she was me. She was actually me! I was stunned by the reality of it. To be able to finally accept that "beautiful" part of me was overwhelming.

Then, it was as if three little girls about eight years old, arm in arm, were skipping along the floor beside me. I will never forget their squeals of delight as we received the gold medal.

It was my time to dance.

It was so much more for me than just fun. The true victory could not be seen by any bystander. The growth of self-worth and acceptance were more vital than any award a competition could give me. I never knew I could look sophisticated, glamorous, elegant, or exotic with a healthy sense of femininity and sexuality. Sexuality I never knew I could have. Never knew it was okay to have. Never

It was my time to dance. John Bogan, my instructor, and I stopped for a quick pose before dancing in a competition in Acapulco. My coach, David Klaus, and I competed in another international contest in New Orleans.

knew it was an important, healthy part of being alive.

The months passed in a whirl of working, studying, and dancing.

Dr. Danylchuk, Lynette, and I were a good team. We had made a commitment to our clients and to each other. It was a stimulating atmosphere but also very hard work. We became so busy that nearly all our time together was spent in conversation regarding clients.

At night, Dr. Danylchuk had Lynette to talk to. I had no one. Professional client confidentiality had to be maintained. I had several new friends, John, and Bill, a handsome guy I had met at the dance studio. But I could share with them only a little of the pressures and concerns I was experiencing.

I ignored increasing fatigue and blotches on my hands and face for a long time. Finally, I decided to get the annoying patches examined by a doctor. I assumed he would give me an ointment or pills and they would be gone. Instead, he ordered blood tests.

The same morning the Challenger went down, the lab results came in. Lupus. My rocket containing all my hopes and dreams exploded that day. Lupus? I knew someone with lupus. She was bedfast.

A robot looking like me tended to my clients that day. The following day, the doctor explained the next steps.

"Lupus is a chronic disease that affects the body's immune system. It has no known cure." But he quickly added, "You'll have no problem living a long, healthy life if you take care of yourself. To start with, you need to get nine to ten hours of sleep a night and an hour's nap in the afternoon, and you must reduce your stress to an absolute minimum."

I choked back laughter. "Do you have any idea what I do? It would be easier for you to tell me to fly to the moon without a rocket than to adhere to that."

I left the office with not much more hope than when I went in. I walked to a small cafe, ordered a tall glass of iced tea, and sat at my favorite table next to the window. I watched the people walk by, all of them unaware of the fear I faced. Slowly, my thoughts settled down and began to form logical questions. *If I have only a few productive months or years left, what do I want to accomplish in that time? What's really most important to me?*

The answers to my questions came instantly. *Write my books: one of my own personal experience, one about my theory, and then the story of the men of the SOTP; teach my Scindo Syndrome Theory to mental health professionals; and start a foundation to train therapists.*

How in the world am I going to have time to do all this, work with the men at the prison, do therapy with clients at the center, travel and speak, and finish my Ph.D. program?

This answer came more slowly, over a period of days and through many tears. I gradually started to terminate my clients at the center, planning to cease my clinical work by the end of the year.

Life took on a certain dragging slowness. Early one Saturday, against my better judgment, I agreed to see a client. The frantic woman seemed to need emergency help. Although exhausted after she left, I decided to stay and catch up on office work.

Hours later, the phone rang. Without thinking, I answered it instead of letting the machine pick it up. The voice on the other end took me by surprise. It was George, from the prison: George, who had slipped soundlessly away after the first presentation; George, who reappeared during my second visit to the prison and became one of my most avid supporters.

I spilled out my recent stresses, the lupus, my decision to leave the center, the hectic pace of my life.

There was a long pause at the end of my narrative. George's voice, deep and mellow, was gentle. "And what's all that busyness trying to cover up?"

Taken aback, I said, "Damn you, George! You've had too much therapy."

George told me how concerned everyone had been about me since they had heard of my lupus. He said, "We all love you, lady. You're so important to each one of us. Please take care of yourself."

I hung up the phone, laid my head on the desk, and wept. *Lord, only you could have caused this man, a convicted rapist in a prison over a thousand miles away, to call me at the time when I need it the most, to let me know that someone cared about me.*

As I reached for the tissue box, I thought of the money George had spent on the call. The men in prison make only ten to twenty-five cents an hour. George's call probably cost him more than a week's wages. *What a special gift.*

As I thought about George, my mind drifted to

the other male friends in my life: some married or living with someone, some gay, young, or in prison. I started laughing with the irony of it all. All were unavailable, "safe" men. More than that, the "old Marilyn" would never have allowed some of them as friends.

My life had changed so much. Todd had remarried. My father had passed away suddenly. A car accident had put Missy in bed for several months and now she also was about to marry. My car had caught on fire. A burglar had recently robbed me of some valued possessions. Stress? I would throw the stress test into the nervous breakdown range. Yet I felt like I was doing very well. If all those things had happened six years before, I would have been bedfast with terrible pain.

But I am not bedfast! I have not even had a headache! I haven't had any pain medication, except during my surgery, since September 1980. I'm having some difficulties, but I'm surviving. Not only am I surviving, but I feel like I am really beginning to live!

♦ ♦ ♦

Having lupus became a positive factor in my life. It forced me to redefine my priorities and goals and made me set healthy boundaries—boundaries I don't think I could have set without being required to do so. While I realize now it has been for my good, for most of 1986 I did not feel that way.

Getting started on my writing seemed impossible. Judith Briles, a close friend from the National Speakers Association and an author of several books, became a mentor for me. She consistently held me accountable by asking, "Are you setting aside time to write?"

Unfortunately, my lupus continued to escalate until I realized I would have to resign from my Ph.D. program, in addition to ceasing my clinical work. I struggled and fought the decision. I had never been a quitter. Walking away from my schooling and the center was devastating.

I would not have survived without Bill, my new friend from the studio. Both recently divorced, we enjoyed spending time together in what eventually became a unique relationship.

His strong masculinity, combined with gentleness and sensitivity, was new to me. He helped me work through the pain of leaving school and the counseling center; he held me as I cried; he used his skills as a CPA to devise a plan whereby I could mortgage my house and sell some of my art to provide funds to live on while I wrote my books and prepared my training seminars.

Bill was several years younger than I, but our personalities and interests meshed, our minds ran on similar tracks. Bill had no problem with a strong, successful woman. He became as excited about my work as I was. Often when I returned from Arizona, he would greet me with, "Has Joey made his parole yet? What about George?"

He never turned away when my Sobbing Hurting Child pulled me back into my old pain. He not only listened to me, he heard me. We disagreed, often. But instead of blowing up in anger or walking away, he was almost always the first to say, "We need to sit down and talk." He was committed to his own emotional growth, and his enthusiasm regarding my theoretical concepts encouraged me more than once.

Most of all, he allowed me to be me; he encouraged me to do so. My therapy time with Dr. Danylchuk had helped me find my Original Feeling Child. My time with Bill taught that emerging child to love and helped her to grow. His Original Feeling Child and mine ran hand in hand over the hilltops. We helped each other climb the rocks, jump the crevices, and scale a precipice, just to see what was on the other side.

Even though neither of us had experienced a special relationship like this before, our personal goals gradually took us in separate directions. We began a spiral of joy and pain, intimacy and withdrawal. After many tries, we finally said good-bye.

Our relationship forced me to realize I still had some major mountains to climb on my healing journey. I had spent hundreds of hours in therapy on one hour of my life, the attack. Yet I had spent years in a marriage which had been basically dysfunctional for a long time. As I interacted with Bill, I started to understand how much my fear of being controlled, plus my old codependency issues, still affected me. I began to face my fears and to work actively on resolving them.

My relationship with my family had improved greatly. My mother and I talked now. I felt loved and supported. I was delighted to see that Jinger's and Missy's children were classic examples of an Original Feeling Child. Even Todd seemed more sensitive to me after his second marriage ended in divorce; he reestablished his bond with our children and grand-

*My grandchildren, BJ, Jannell, and
Ashley (clockwise) are all certifiable
Original Feeling Children.*

*My children, Jinger, and son-in-law Brad (top) and
Missy (bottom) learning to grow into Feeling Adults.*

children and became more supportive and understanding. Some of our church friends, who formerly were critical, became aware of and responsive to issues regarding childhood abuse. I was pleased to receive invitations to present my Scindo Syndrome training seminars in Kansas. Gradually the old ways were changing, for all of us.

I also realized it was time to mend the most important relationship in my life: to become friends with God again. For several years I felt as if He and I were sitting in the same room but in opposite corners. Occasionally we would wave at each other. Actually, it was okay. He knew I needed the time to be angry, and I knew He said it was okay—like a child who goes in her room and storms at her parent but knows the parent will be there waiting patiently when the child comes out. And I did start to come out. I began to hold God's hand again, but in a new and liberating way.

As part of my spiritual journey, I decided to return to Czechslovakia, a pilgrimage to Prague. For many years one of my goals had been to visit Milos Sole and his parishioners again. For ten days, Milos, his wife, and I traversed Bohemia, Moravia, and Slovakia—meeting in tiny homes, in rural churches, in large churches, in country cabins. People touched my face, and they wept. I prayed with them, and I also cried. I was at home—behind the barbed wire fence, sixteen strands high and six strands deep, surrounding that country. While the situation there had improved somewhat since my last visit nine years prior, I was still affected by the enormity of the difference between their world and mine. Yet, again, I was tempted to stay. Milos's smile and unconditional love made life bearable there for so many.

Upon my return to California, I wanted to find a church home, one that was conservative in doctrine but liberal in love and understanding, one whose pastors were honest about their *own* difficulties and failures. I did not know if such a place existed, but Bill recommended one he thought I would enjoy. On my first visit, the pastor's sermon was entitled, "The Dark Night of the Soul." His compassion and understanding of deep emotional pain touched me greatly. As the congregation stood to sing the closing hymn, the words of "Amazing Grace" reached in and wrapped themselves around my inner children. Instead of crying, they smiled.

My children and I were beginning to understand just a sliver of what grace and forgiveness are really all about.

♦ 18 ♦

All My Victims

I had resigned from my Ph.D. program and ceased my clinical work at the center, but I held on to my prison work. Over the years several of the men of the SOTP had become my spiritual mainstay and were among my strongest supporters.

But not everyone was enthusiastic about my being there. Jack, in his first visit to the group, sat straight in his chair, the veins standing out on his neck as he cast his violent words into the air. "I'm really pissed! We don't need another person coming in here, pointing a finger at us, telling us how bad we are." He jumped up from his chair and blurted, "I'm sick of people telling us we'll always be offenders, that sex offenders never change."

Bart's voice cut through the room. "Hey, why don't you just cool it and let the lady continue."

Jack whirled around to face Bart. "Don't front *me* off, man!"

Quietly, yet firmly, Bart continued, "I, for one, am getting a lot out of what she says. If you'll just listen for a while, I think you'll decide she isn't what you think she is."

Jack sat down, glum, skeptical, and silent.

Words of sadness filled the room. Men, abused as children, revealed the horrendous stories of their past. In the corner, a bearded man sat silently during the entire time of sharing. His body began to shake, completely enveloped in sorrow.

"I didn't know I was hurting my little girl so much. If I'd only known." Tears drowned words as he realized how much pain he had caused his daughter. Quietly I got up and walked over to him.

"It's okay to let it come, Sam." I gently helped him to his feet and wrapped my arms around him until his sobs ceased.

Sam looked at me in sorrow and confusion as he said, "How can you be here with us, knowing what we've done?"

As I returned to my chair I answered, "I wouldn't be able to if I hadn't spent hour after hour beating the hell out of my offenders with a racquet on a mat in a therapy room. During that time I finally was able to express my rage toward my offenders. As a result, I don't transfer that anger on to you. Instead, I can see you as valued human beings. That doesn't mean I condone what you, or my offenders, did. You still have to be accountable for your actions. It means that now I separate the deed from the man, without having my judgment influenced by buried rage."

Jack leaned forward, speaking to me. "I want to apologize. I was wrong. You aren't any of those things I said. I'm sorry. Thanks for all you're doing for us."

Next to him, William nodded in agreement. "Because of what you, Dr. Mazen, and all the staff have done, I can talk to my sons better. I want to be a good father. I don't want them to end up like I did."

I listened to him as he continued. I wondered at his strength of spirit. Having served sixteen years of a life sentence for rape, with no possibility of parole, I had first thought he would not care about bettering himself, but I was wrong. He was working hard in therapy, and he had received his Associate in Arts Degree with courses in law and psychology. Many men in prison, faced with long term sentences, turn to drugs, alcohol, and violence. William, an outstanding exception, was one of the most respected inmates on the yard. Admired by blacks, hispanics, and whites, he was a man who walked with dignity and grace. His strong faith shone in his face. Unlike the "Bible thumpers," his sincerity and genuine caring drew people to him.

William's commitment to being the best role model possible to his sons had yielded excellent results. Two of the four had graduated from college, with the fourth still in high school. William's sons had been regular visitors and his wife had visited him nearly every week during the past sixteen years.

As the session ended, I stood by the door, giving each man a hug. An action once so difficult had now become an important thread in the tapestry of my healing.

At the end of the line stood William. Quietly he approached me and hesitated as I touched him. As my arms encircled his shoulders, I felt him shudder and clutch at his chest. He sucked sharp gasps through his teeth.

I stepped back a half step. "William, are you okay?"

Several seconds passed as he grasped at his T-shirt where his heart pounded furiously, still unable to speak.

"Just take a deep breath," I encouraged. "It'll be all right. Let's sit down a minute."

He slumped into the chair. I placed my arms around him as tears brimmed in his incredulous eyes. "Oh Marilyn, you just became all my victims." He shuddered again. "I didn't think any one of them could ever touch me. Especially not with a feeling of forgiveness."

My eyes searched his dark face. I whispered, "William, were all of your victims white?"

The answer came softly. "Yes, yes."

Taking his hands in mine, I hesitated, then continued, "William, I'm going to tell you something I've never told anyone in this prison before: my offenders were black."

His gaze flew to meet mine as I said softly, "William, look at me and see all your victims. I forgive you for them. And as I look at you, I see all my offenders."

I stammered as I said the next difficult words. "Today, I . . . I forgive them, too."

The powerful healing of that moment drifted through the walls of the old metal trailer, out across the dusty fields, and over the top of the razor-wire fence, carrying its message of forgiveness far beyond the boundaries of the physical shells that encased us—a message of forgiveness and freedom, for William, and for me.

That evening, I walked down the dirt streets of

the small desert town of Florence and turned into a little Mexican restaurant. As I sat to eat, my mind was racing with the day's events. I poked at my refried beans, reminding myself that not all offenders in prison were like William. Even in the SOTP there had been failures. I had been disappointed and somewhat disillusioned when I had encountered men who refused to be committed to change and dropped out of the program, some who used drugs, got into fights, or had other infractions and were "rolled up," or sent back behind the walls. *But those who did try, those who did work hard and kept themselves clean, how would I feel if one of them re-offended?*

My thoughts continued as I started walking to my familiar room at the Blue Mist Motel. The sound of electric guitars echoed from the doorway of the corner bar, filling the streets.

Turning the corner, the falling darkness pushed me away from the occasional hedges and trees and into the street in front of the old houses. Brash young "machos" cruised by in their pickups, their stereos beating at unbearable levels. Rifles rested in racks behind their heads.

Ugly thoughts slithered through my mind, thoughts that brought fear on its rattling tail. I thought of my friend in San Francisco who recently called me in tears, telling of a robbery and brutal rape she had just experienced. My anger towards her offender was enormous. I took these thoughts, forming ideas and questions for the men at the prison. Somehow I needed to balance my concern and caring for them with the hard facts that they were capable of re-offending.

I did not go to the prison to coddle the inmates. I did not go to pacify them and excuse them for their actions. I wanted this horrible chain of abuse to end somewhere. I gathered my courage to touch the spot in them I knew would be painful.

The next morning, I stood in front of them, smiling solemnly. "It haunts me, as I wonder if anyone who has been through SOTP will re-offend. I don't want you to ever get so satisfied with your changes and growth that you become complacent and forget the possibility that you too could become a recidivism statistic."

I began to describe the streets of the town lying only a few hundred yards from the door of the trailer. I described my walk the evening before, being honest about my uneasiness in being alone.

"I want you to imagine something with me, allowing yourself to feel your response. Suppose one of those boys, cruising around last night, forced me to go with him into the desert where he brutally raped me . . ."

The men began to squirm and fidget. Muscles tensed, jaws tightened.

"Then suppose that young man was arrested and just happened to be sentenced to the Arizona State Prison at Florence. One day he walks into this trailer and asks to sign up for the SOTP. What would you do?"

"He'd never live long enough to ask!"

Faces flushed as hostility bristled in the room. Then, almost in unison, shoulders sagged as recognition glinted in lowered eyes.

"I guess he's no different than any of us. He'd

deserve a chance to change through this program, too."

I continued. "Imagine the same scene. Only this time the man who rapes me is a man who has spent two years in this trailer going through the SOTP and is now on parole. He is caught and sent back to Florence and he wants to re-enter the program. What would you do?"

The rage was more intense than the first time.

"I'd gladly kill him!"

"He'd deserve to die."

I looked each man directly in the eye and asked, "Why are you so much tougher on him than on the first man?"

Several voices harshly declared, "Because he *knew* better!"

Suddenly their faces looked as if they had been slugged below the belt. Each man winced as one exclaimed, "You really set us up with that one!"

"I'm not done yet. Why should it matter to you if the person who was sexually abused was *me*? I chose myself for the victim because everyone here has known me approximately the same amount of time and under similar circumstances. I could have said the victim was one of your wives or daughters or sisters or mothers, or just some unknown woman or child who unfortunately happened to be walking down that street. Why should it matter who it was?"

"Yeah. I guess we need to be outraged whenever any innocent person gets hurt. Not just someone we love."

I looked around the room. "We've discussed how hard you can be on yourselves when you blow it around here. I've encouraged you to lighten up. But there's one thing in which you never want to blow it. And that's re-offending.

"I really do care about each of you. I'm sorry to be so rough on you, but I don't ever want to see you back here once you're finally free. You've worked too long for that."

The men nodded in painful agreement. I touched on a fear they all had. They wanted to believe they would never offend again. But they knew their weakness. They knew the statistics. Each man dealt with an inner torment, yet they appreciated what I said, even through the pain.

A man spoke for the feelings of the rest of them. "I didn't want to think that the danger of re-offending had anything to do with what happened to me as a kid. I went around for months refusing to believe I had anything repressed in my past. I thought what you told us about yourself was a big story. Then one day I thought, 'Why would that lady lie to me? She must be telling the truth.' But then I had to deal with all my own childhood pain. All of the anger and the hurt you stirred up inside of me."

Another man spoke up. "Hey man. I want to see us all change. PERMANENTLY."

I wished the same for them. I knew the change could not come overnight. It took hours and hours of hard, painful work: hours of uncovering and dealing with the abusive experiences of their childhood years that created the foundation for their offender-behavior; hours of accepting responsibility for their own abusive actions; hours of attending classes to help build new, appropriate modes of behavior, classes on values and decisions, on communication, sexuality, and self-esteem.

I had been the "bottle opener," the one who helped them take the top off their pools of pain. The real work was done by others. The men of the SOTP were fortunate to have Hila Jo Hawk and Theron Weldy, who taught the education classes and helped facilitate the couples groups, Dr. Mazen and the rest of the dedicated staff who were willing to give hours of time and emotion to help tear down the old and restructure the new—not only within the prison, but during the crucial follow-up period after the men were finally released.

I continued to go back to the prison. The changed lives kept me coming back. Then it was over. The Department of Corrections announced the program was being moved to Tucson despite many protests from the staff and participants.

Only a few of the men with whom I worked qualified to move with the program. The majority would have to stop their therapy, no matter what painful issue they happened to be working on.

I returned for a final week of personal sessions with each man in the program. My feelings of frustration and anger were mixed with a deep sense of sorrow and loss.

I was profoundly moved when Bart responded to my feelings by saying, "We were all very angry at first. But you know, we are really lucky. We have had a chance at change and growth almost no one else in prison, anywhere, has ever had. Even though we may not be done with our therapy and classes yet, we're still strongly committed to passing on what we've learned to as many people as possible."

Bart excitedly related how that was already happening in the life of Joey, now out on parole—he was enrolled in college and working part-time as a counselor in a drug-abuse center. As Bart and I talked, the door opened and William stepped in, his smile bright in his dark face.

William and I walked to the other end of the trailer and entered the small therapy room. As he settled himself on an old metal chair, William began to share how his life had changed since we first met and he started in SOTP: he was learning to genuinely communicate with his wife and sons; he was writing to legislators about prison conditions; he continued to work with his own victimized Sobbing Hurting Child by feeling the child's pain and by beginning to reparent himself; but most of all, he was aware of the grief and pain he had caused his victims, and God, as a result of his crimes.

Unaware that night had descended, I was startled when the guard looked in to take count. As the door closed, I reached across the table to clasp William's hands. "William, you are special to me. You've been such an important part of my healing journey."

Our hands joined across the table. My eyes filled with tears as I watched the muscles in his arm tense and vibrate until the tension seemed to explode.

Tears streaked down his face. "I really just feel like I don't deserve this from you. I don't deserve what God has given to me. I know God's word says, 'All have sinned and come short of the glory of God,' but . . ."

Suddenly moans of grief erupted, and he buried his head in his arms and wept for a lifetime of pain and lost years. I slipped next to him and put my arms around the man and the child.

I whispered, "William, do you know God has forgiven you?"

He nodded.

"Do you know I have forgiven you?" Again, a slight nod.

"William, when will you be able to forgive yourself?"

Slowly he wiped his tears, "But all the hurt I've caused . . ."

"I know, I know, but it takes time, and look how far you've come."

Clasping my hands he stammered, "What can I ever do to repay . . ."

"William, the greatest gift you could give me is to learn to love and forgive yourself. You are a person of worth no matter what happened in your past."

Bart's sudden knock on the door signaled time had run out. I took a farewell glance around the trailer, the rooms where so many men became my friends. *Isn't it funny that in this place I once again learned that men can be sensitive and caring, understanding and respectful. Who would have ever thought that I, a rape victim, would feel the safest, the most protected, the most understood, the most accepted, the most cherished, and the most loved when I am in a little trailer in a dusty prison yard, in a room filled with rapists and child molesters.*

I began to scoop up my scattered papers and tapes as Bart and William picked up the styrofoam cups—the last remnants of today's final group. A few unexpected tears joined the coffee stains on the cups as they threw them in the battered trash can.

Bart finished turning out the lights of the trailer as William gathered up my video equipment. We walked silently to my car, glad for the protective covering of night for our tears. William's hand reached through the car window and gently touched my shoulder as he said, "Blessings on you, dear friend."

I drove past the guard and out the gate. With eyes filled with sadness and awe, I watched Bart and William in my rearview mirror as they walked slowly to the old Quonset huts in which they lived.

They were free men, even though their physical bodies remained imprisoned behind that razor-wire fence, in a prison that had been their entire world for sixteen years. And if that prison continues to be their entire world for the rest of their lives, *they will always be free men.*

♦ 19 ♦

The Real World,
The Real War

My frontier has been like the West of the 1800's: sometimes exciting, sometimes dangerous: a path filled with detours, and even some dead ends. I have felt lost, frustrated, and afraid. The nights were often long and lonely, but morning is finally dawning for me—a morning filled with freedom:

> Freedom from pain medication; freedom, most of the time, from physical pain, at least for now.
> Freedom to feel, with awareness that this freedom brings with it the possibility of emotional pain—-pain that is real, pain that lets me know I'm *alive*; and the freedom, to, at last, know it is okay to care of my emotional wounds.
> Freedom to be me, to be a multi-facted person, totally aware of, and valuing, all the parts of me: my Controlling Child, my Sobbing Hurting Child, my Original Feeling Child, and my Feeling Adult.

As I continue my journey I can look across the hills and see I am not alone. On other mountain tops I see my friends: Dr. Ralph Earle, past national president of the American Association for Marriage and Family Therapy; Dr. Peter Danylchuk and his wife, Lynette, providing therapy for adult victims of abuse at Restoration Therapy Center; Dr. Sandy Mazen continuing to do therapy with released offenders and their families; Hila Jo Hawk and Theron Weldy, heading the Sex Offender Treatment Program for the state of Kansas; Dr. Arlys Norcross, a specialist in the treatment of abused adults and children; Beverly James, internationally known author and seminar leader on treatment for childhood abuse; Rich Buhler, well-known radio personality and author who champions the work of uncovering buried childhood trauma; Dr. and Mrs. Hank Giaretto, founders of Parents United for families of incest; my fellow members of Childhelp USA, one of the finest organizations regarding child abuse prevention, treatment, and research in the country; and the memory of Virginia Satir, a pioneer in the field of family therapy who honored me with her friendship and the opportunity to co-present with her.

I see so many others. Persons whose books I've read, tapes I've heard, and seminars I've attended. Some are close friends; others I've yet to meet. Persons whom I've silently, and not so silently, cheered on. *We are not alone in this war.* Some are on the hilltops, but there are thousands who are in the trenches: therapists, educators, parents—people who care about hurting children, people as important as those who are more visible.

And almost everyone is a wounded soldier. No one is the Original Feeling Child he or she was created to be. Everyone has a Sobbing Hurting Child of some size or intensity. The child's pain doesn't have to be from sexual or physical abuse. Emotional abuse and the lack of love can be just as devastating to a child. Recognizing that your Sobbing Hurting Child exists, paying attention to that child and its pain, is scary, yet so necessary if you want to become a whole, healthy, fully functioning Feeling Adult.

Change begins within yourself, as you become an intimate friend with all the parts of yourself: by releasing and reparenting your Sobbing Hurting Child, by reclaiming your delightful Original Feeling Child, and by recognizing how your Controlling Child has kept the other two buried, maybe for many years.

The path toward wholeness is made one step at a time. Your path probably will be very different from mine. I don't believe that intensive therapy like I experienced is necessary for everyone. Find the path that's right for you.

Don't hesitate to seek help on your healing journey. There are many qualified therapists who are deeply concerned for hurting persons. More and more professionals are seeking specialized training regarding abuse. Crisis centers, shelters, and hotlines are available in every city and in many towns. Support groups and Twelve-Step programs can be found everywhere, even in some of the most conservative churches. Hope for healing is greater now than ever before.

For many of you, a healing journey may also include a spiritual one. Like me, you may need time to work through your anger and slowly start to rebuild your trust in God again. This doesn't happen alone. In my own journey, I feel God provided people to be vessels through which He showed His love for me. It also took some major re-evaluations of my childhood boundaries. Your journey may take you far from your own childhood boundaries or perhaps you will stay within those boundaries and change them from within.

Can everyone change? I doubt it. I am not a pollyanna. I balance my feelings with reality and know that for some, change will never come. Some will stay in their destructive patterns forever. Even with the possibility of change, not everyone wants to make the commitment, to take the effort and time, or to give up the power, or to feel the pain. Sometimes the pain is more comfortable than the fear of facing its source.

Recognizing that one's Sobbing Hurting Child exists is a lifelong task. I found I needed to accept my Hurting Child as a permanent part of me just as naturally as I would if I had an amputated leg and walked with an artificial limb. If I had a prosthesis, I would know I had to be careful walking down stairways or stepping off curbs, to be careful when I went around a protruding shelf.

In the same manner, I now am fully aware of things that can knock the legs out from under my own Sobbing Hurting Child. She reacts instantly to the sound of a small child screaming in terror. More than once I've had to leave a grocery store because of a lost child. I do not stay around and try . to tough it out. I just leave.

When my father died, the feeling of "abandonment" caught me totally unprepared. In the hospital as I said my final good-bye to him, and then three days later at the funeral, I experienced extremely painful spontaneous regressions. The response was so violent, I was unable to keep from being pulled off my cliff and back into my attack. I was embarrassed and vulnerable. I realize the people who watched may have felt I was prostrate with grief over my father, some may have understood it was my child in the attack, or others may have reacted in disdain at my inability to be "strong" and keep my emotions under control.

Yet, spontaneous regressions such as this are not uncommon for other persons beside me. And these regressions will become more and more common. I encounter them—many of them—every time I speak on the subject of childhood abuse.

Today the activation of repressed trauma happens every day as unidentified victims read newspapers and magazines, and watch TV and movies. Child abuse is the topic everywhere. Consequently, multitudes of hidden Sobbing Children are responding to what they see and hear. If this happens to you, or to someone you know and love, do not panic. It's a natural release of that child's pain. The best thing you can do is to lovingly hold that child in an adult body and let that child know it's now safe to feel.

To acknowledge our own woundedness is the first step toward healing, yet breaking the chain of abuse also involves the necessity of looking at the issue in a much broader fashion.

When I first started to work as a therapist and realized we were victims of "another war," I thought we were waging a war only against child abuse. Now I realize it is far more than that. It is a war against the breeding grounds for all abuse. It is a war against any ideology and/or system which encourages

- the supremacy of a particular race, creed, or sex,
- the physical, sexual, and/or emotional abuse of any person,
- the suppression of a person's individuality and dignity,
- the denial of the worth and value of every human being.

A therapist in West Virginia who attended one of my training seminars recently wrote to me and included an article by Elie Wiesel, the Nobel Prize Winner for Peace. In it Mr. Wiesel states:

> In time of war, they try to make us believe that anyone who is not our brother is our enemy: We are forbidden to listen too closely to our hearts, to be compassionate or even to let ourselves be carried away by our imaginations. If the soldier were to consider the enemy a potential victim (of war) and therefore capable of weeping, or despairing, of dying . . . the relationship between them would be changed. Every effort is made, therefore, to limit, even stifle, his humane impulses, his imagination and his capacity to experience a feeling of brotherhood toward his fellow man . . . (H)enceforth war will be without glory and without a future, it will leave no conquerors, but only victims. Wars fought between countries are started by persons who want to conquer and to force other persons into the aggressor's ideological boundaries, by persons who cannot respect another's right to his or her

own beliefs and values. These wars are fought by persons who see someone outside their boundaries as the enemy.

When we can see our enemy as a child who feels loneliness and fear, a child who knows pain, who cries, who can bleed—then we will begin to change the world. If we can look beneath that pain and see the Original Feeling Child that that person was created to be, then we are no longer enemies, we are only human beings joined together within one boundary.

When we see the child in others, we will replace hate with forgiveness, prejudice with understanding, bigotry with acceptance, disdain with compassion, and arrogance with equality.

It does not mean approval of evil deeds or violent, abusive actions. It does mean learning to understand the cause. I have listened to many boys and men who have committed horrible crimes. And I have listened to the offenses, often more horrendous, that were committed against them when they were children.

To look at offenders with an attitude reflecting a balance somewhere between apathy and a lynch mob is a new concept for most persons. As I finished a television appearance recently, a man roared up to me and yelled, "You don't know what these monsters do to their victims!" I replied, "Bull— — I don't. I'll match my pain to yours, hour for hour any day. I think I've earned the right to speak on behalf of some of these men. If I can forgive them, how can you do less?"

It is my belief that we will finally begin to break the chain of abuse—to win a major battle in this war—when we are able to look within the abuser and find the abused, to find out why a child turns from victim to victimizer, to understand that offenders don't "just happen," and to believe that change *is* possible for many offenders—if therapy is provided by qualified, caring professionals, and if the offender is willing to take responsibility for his or her past actions and is willing to face his or her own pain as the process of change takes place. Prison terms for offenders, without specific treatment which deals with the root cause of their pain and anger, are ineffectual and costly. A recent comment in the *Washington Post* stated that building more prisons to stop crime is like building more hospitals to stop AIDS.

I believe in change because I have seen the results, not only in my life, but in the lives of multitudes of others. Yet, I am fully aware of the intensity of the war in which we find ourselves. To keep myself from becoming overwhelmed by the enormity of the battles ahead, I have a plaque over my desk which reads:

You save the whole world
One child at a time.

I am dedicated to saving that child, be it in the body of a small boy or girl, or be it imprisoned within the frame of an adult man or woman.

The God in whom I believe states in both the Old and the New Testament, "I have come to bind up the broken hearted, to proclaim liberty to the captives, and the opening of the prison to them that are bound."

There are certain questions that I am often asked:

"Was your journey hard?"
Absolutely.
"Was it painful?"
Definitely.
"Did it take long?"
A lifetime.
"Was it worth it?"

This last is a question I have often asked myself.

What about that late afternoon so many years ago when an innocent child walked unsuspecting down a shrublined snowy street? What about the terror and pain, the incredible agony of splitting and burying that tortured child, the internal and emotional suicide? Would I go back to age eight? Would I go back and ride the bus again, only this time watching for my stop? This time I could get off at the right place. I could avoid the attack, avoid the years of physical and emotional pain, avoid the hours of painful therapy, avoid the divorce, avoid the devastation of rejection and non-support—all of it. What would I do if I had a second chance? Would I do it all again? Was it worth it?

From my hilltop, I can look over my shoulder and see the prison at Florence the way it looked the last night I left: the silhouette of the guard turrets, their shadows falling long across the silent yard; the moon glistening and reflecting off the ribbon wire as it encircles my friends bound within that place.

Yes, I'd do it all again. It was worth it all. To see

the changed lives, to give hope to other hurting hearts, to receive a letter like the one slipped to me by one of the men of the SOTP as he said his final goodbye.

It read:

Dear Marilyn,

Each time you come down here, I see your genuine love and concern for us, a bunch of hard-headed cons. You stand at the door as we leave and give me a hug. Me, a rapist. You, a victim. It makes me feel like a real person. A free person. I never thought I would ever deserve to feel like that.

You helped change our lives. You believed in us and showed by example that you loved us. Our forever thanks.

◆ ◆ ◆

Today I, too, am free.

I am no longer a sobbing, hurting child on the black, dirty ground; I am *alive and increasingly well*. I feel that God looks at my "children" and smiles.

My path might continue to be difficult, but I hope my journey has created a new frontier, a legacy created out of my child's pain: a frontier of freedom where children, and adults, are no longer imprisoned victims of war.

My Original Child beckons you to follow—to find your own unique path for *your* healing journey.

Epilogue

The Circle Is Complete

December 26, 1989. I sat in my mother's tiny apartment, watching her as she talked. She looked frail as we discussed the phone call she had received the night before. Her last remaining sister, Rozella, had suffered a heart attack and was not expected to live through the day.

It had been twenty-seven degrees below zero in Kansas that week, and I tried to discourage Mother from attending the funeral. Her arthritis was severe, and she was catching a cold, but she really wanted to go. My sister, Mary Sue, her husband, Wayne, and their twelve-year-old son, Josh, had offered to drive her in their new van. I told her I would fly to Wichita and join them in Marion for the funeral. However, when she said she didn't expect me to attend, I was relieved.

I was exhausted, and I didn't have any winter clothes with me, certainly not any appropriate for a funeral. I had come to Phoenix with only holiday clothes fit for the seventy-to eighty-degree weather. I was scheduled to leave early the next morning to drive to the prison in Florence. I had received special permission to do follow-up work there with the men of the former SOTP, and I had made plans to meet with several of the men who were out on parole, and their wives, during the next few days before I returned to California.

That sunny Tuesday afternoon I visited with Mother for several hours. Once it was settled that she was going to Kansas, and I was not, we then reflected on how much we had enjoyed the weekend (prior to the news about Aunt Rozella.) The entire family had attended Christmas services together and spent Christmas Eve and Christmas Day enjoying Josh, B.J., Janell, and the two-year-old antics of Missy's little live wire, Ashley. Even Todd had joined us. Mother was glad that Todd and I now were able to be friends and that he had renewed his relationship with Jinger and Missy. Mother's family was the delight of her life. She seemed at peace and glad that she did not need to "worry" about a major crisis in any of our lives at that moment.

Mother brought me a cup of hot tea as we discussed the new gallery that Jinger, Brad and I opened last year in Scottsdale and the nostalgia we felt while watching B.J. and Janell help during art shows. Mother was pleased to hear that I had received my approval as a psychological assistant and could resume my clinical work. She seemed genuinely supportive as we talked of my plan to complete my Ph.D. program and of my recent decision to move to the San Diego area. We finished our hot tea, and I cautioned her about the icy streets in Kansas as I hugged her good-bye.

Three days later, on Friday evening, Jinger and Brad were waiting for me as I walked through the door of their house. Jinger was in tears. They had just received a phone call from Mary Sue and Wayne in Kansas.

At her request, they had taken Mother directly to the funeral home when they arrived in Marion that afternoon. With Mary Sue, Wayne and Josh beside her, Mother had walked up to the casket of her sister, the sister who shared her same birthday: Rozella was eighty-two; Mother was seventy-five. As she reached out to touch her sister's hand, Mother suddenly touched her own temple saying, "Oh, I have a terrible pain in my head. I've never had a headache like this before." Her legs crumpled, and Wayne dashed to call an ambulance.

On the frantic drive to the Marion hospital, Mary Sue sat by Mother's side. In less than fifteen minutes from her first pain, Mother stopped breathing. The ambulance attendants were able to revive her, but the doctors gave Mary Sue and Wayne little hope that she would survive without being severely handicapped, physically and mentally. She had suffered a massive brain hemorrhage. Her only chance was surgery by a specialist in Wichita, sixty miles away. Arrangements were made for her to be transported there immediately.

I flew all night and arrived at the airport at half past eight on Saturday morning. All my old "buttons" were pushed as I read the sign above the terminal gate: "Welcome to Wichita."

Wayne greeted me with a compassionate hug, and we climbed into the van and started toward the hospital. It was cold and misting. I felt numb as I watched the street signs flash by: "Kellogg," "Douglas," all familiar to my eight-year-old child.

As Wayne drove, he told me that the results of a

CAT scan had revealed damage so great that surgery was no longer an option for my mother. Now it was "only a matter of hours."

Tears jumped to my eyes. I quickly wiped them away. *It's not "safe" for me to feel, not here, not now.* I was very aware that from the moment Jinger and Brad met me at the door the night before, my Controlling Child had clicked into action and now was struggling to maintain control—that "emotional shock mechanism" about which I write and teach was fully active.

Standing by my mother's bedside looking at her nearly lifeless form, I felt totally split—as if part of me was off to the side just watching as the rest of me stood helplessly holding my mother's hand. I realized I was asking and answering questions in a mind separated from my feelings. I was simply going through the motions of doing whatever I needed to do. As I became more and more aware of the necessary role of my Controlling Child during the intensity of the traumatic situation, I found myself grateful for how appropriately strong she was—for the moment anyway.

Within a few hours, after several tests, the doctor informed us that the blood had ceased flowing to Mother's brain and that she no longer was functioning as a living person. He asked if we wanted him to remove her life-support system. We said yes, knowing that it was what she would have wanted.

Mary Sue, Wayne, Josh, and I all were supportive of each other. As we prepared to say our final good-byes to Mother, I found myself shaking. Memories of my spontaneous regressions when our father died flooded my mind. Mary Sue and Wayne also remembered and were concerned.

Fear and abandonment raged through me and tore at my insides, threatening to engulf me once again. I wasn't at all sure that my Controlling Child could handle this.

I prayed as I fought to keep my Sobbing Hurting Child from pulling me back down into my old pain. *Please Lord, help me to handle my grief as a Feeling Adult— let me feel the pain, but only the pain of today.* I began to plead as the tears started cascading down my face, *Please, please, don't let me be swamped by that terrorized child inside of me.*

At the moment I was feeling the most alone and afraid, God provided something profound. Just as Mary Sue, Wayne, Josh, and I were ready to leave our small, private waiting room and start down the hall toward the intensive care unit, the door opened. We were startled to see the pastor of our home church in Marion. The day before, he had "just happened" to be at the funeral home when my mother was stricken; he also had performed Aunt Rozella's funeral in Marion that afternoon; now, at eleven p.m. on a Saturday night, he was picking up his wife after she had received a chemotherapy treatment for bone cancer at the same hospital in Wichita.

This strong, yet gentle, loving pastor sat and prayed with us and then walked with me to my mother's bedside. I asked him to wait outside the curtain as I said good-bye.

I looked down at my mother's hands, hands all twisted and gnarled from years of painful arthritis, the hands to which my terrified eight-year-old had clung on all those nights when my nightmares were so bad, crying, "Please Momma, just hold my hand and keep me awake so I won't have the dream."

On this night, I leaned over her bed and sobbed, "Momma, Momma, I'm so sorry I've caused you so much pain. I love you so much." As I kissed her, I whispered, "Good-bye for now. I'll see you again soon."

I allowed my tears to flow, but they were the tears of an adult, not of a child. It was the ultimate test: my mother died in Wesley Hospital in Wichita, Kansas, on Hillside Avenue, *only three blocks from the big old white house in which we lived at the time of my attack.*

It was snowing.

Christmas Day, 1989. Mother, Ashley, Missy, Mary Sue, myself, Jinger, and Janell in front.

Acknowledgments

My deep appreciation to:

Todd, for the good years;

to many family members and friends, who shared
their love and concern through their support
and prayers, especially my daughter Jinger and
Missy and Jinger's husband, Brad; my sister
Mary Sue, her husband Wayne and children:
Tim, Randy, Jennifer, and Josh;

everyone in MORE THAN FRIENDS, especially my
own personal group and Barbara, who continue
to show me they are truly more than friends;

Kay, who cared enough to insist that I get help;

Pete, who showed me unconditional love, and
Lynette, for being understanding and
supportive of him;

Babette, who comforted and cared for me, and
Don, for his patience;

Cecil, who paved the way;

Ralph, who continually encourages me and
motivates me to grow;

George, who trusted my concepts and shared his
knowledge;

Florence and Fred, who believed in me and
provided a platform;

Bill, who helped me to love and be a whole person;

Norma, who taught me to value myself;

John, who showed me how to play;

Charlotte, who understands and cares;

Judith, who never gave up on me;

Arlys, who always understands;

Russ, who listens gently;

Janelle and Jeffrey, who widen my horizons;

Steve and Jan, for help above and beyond the call of duty;

Tim, Joe, Barry, Cynthia, Randy, Kate, Beverly, Holliday, Jane, Rosemary, Brenda, Tiba, Barbara, Carolyn, Vivian, Pete, Carmen, Andrew, Rich, Linda, Ray and Blondine for being very special friends;

my clients, who shared their hearts with me;

the men of the Sex Offender Treatment Program at the Arizona State Prison, who had the courage to listen to me and the willingness to change, and Sandy and all the staff, who made my work there possible.

My special appreciation to: my editor and publisher, Mr. Roy M. Carlisle of PageMill Press, whose infinite patience, wisdom, and encouragement made this book possible; to Mary McClellan whose editorial skills and belief in my story helped immeasurably; to Shirley Loffer who polished the final manuscript with unique sensitivity and talent; and to Lissa Halls Johnson, whose words were a gift to this story.

At 54 . . . a Feeling Adult and still growing.

About the Author

Marilyn L. Murray, M.A., is a woman of multiple careers: a respected art dealer; co-founder of the national women's support group, More Than Friends; and now a psychotherapist.

Ms. Murray is nationally recognized as an authority on abuse and its consequences. Her personal presentations and her Scindo Syndrome Theory and Training Seminars have been enthusiastically received throughout the country.

As a specialist in intensive regressive therapy she is associated with New Vistas Therapy Center, Vista, California, and Psychological Counseling Services, Scottsdale, Arizona.

She is also co-owner of the Legacy Gallery, Scottsdale, Arizona.

Ms. Murray is a member of the American Association of Sex Educators, Counselors and Therapists, the National Speakers Association and serves on the late Virginia Satir's ongoing Advisor Board of the Avanta Network.

For information please contact:

Marilyn Murray & Associates
11545 West Bernardo Court, Suite 100
San Diego, California 92128
(619) 592-1511
FAX (619) 451-7781